How Islam Created
The Modern World

© Copyright 2006 AC/1427 AH
amana publications
10710 Tucker Street
Beltsville, MD 20705-2223 USA
Tel. 301-595-5777, 800-660-1777
Fax 301-595-5888, 240-250-3000

Email: amana@amana-corp.com
Website: www.amanapublications.com

First Edition (Hard Cover)
2006 AC/1427 AH

First Edition (Paperback)
2017 AC/1438 AH

Hard Cover: 978-1-59008-043-6
Paperback: 978-1-59008-084-9

Illustrations by Lori Mae Peters

Library of Congress Cataloging-in-Publications Data

Graham, Mark A., 1970-
   How Islam created the modern world / Mark Graham. -- 1st ed.
   p. cm.
   Includes index.
   ISBN 1-59008-043-2
   1. Islam--Universality. 2. Civilization, Western--Islamic influences.
3. Civilization, Islamic--Western influences. 4. Islam--Essence,
genius, nature. 5. East and West. I. Title.
BP170.8.G73 2006
297.09--dc22

                                                          2006012231

Printed by Mega Printing in Turkey

How Islam Created The Modern World

MARK GRAHAM

ILLUSTRATIONS BY LORI MAE PETERS

amana publications

For my parents,
Kenneth and Michele Graham,
who taught me to love the truth
and to keep an open mind.

Contents

Acknowledgements

I have depended on the support, inspiration and generosity of a number of individuals while writing this book. Professor Akbar S. Ahmed wrote me an excellent foreword. My editor Ahmed Osman provided keen insight and guidance. My colleague Anita Lewis included me on her tour of Spain, where I walked the streets of Ibn Rushd's hometown of Cordoba and spent a delightful morning in its beautiful mosque. Jennifer Johnson, another colleague of mine, helped me with acquiring research materials. The courteous staff of Muhlenberg College's Trexler Library provided me with the opportunity to use the library's extensive resources. Lori Mae Peters provided exquisite illustrations for this book. My parents encouraged me from the beginning, and my wife Fauzia and sons, Dean and Zayn, gave me the will and the reason to write what I did. God willing/Inshallah it will do some good.

Foreword

By Akbar S. Ahmed

After September 11, 2001, Muslims have been depicted in the media as "extremists", "terrorists" and "barbarians". People have reduced Islam to "terrorism". Implicit in this view is the perception that Islam as a civilization is not capable of producing anything worthwhile. It allows the easy dehumanization of individual Muslims. It therefore encourages acts of cruelty when individuals are involved–from random acts in the United States to the Abu Ghraib prison in Baghdad, Iraq. It is easy to be cruel to someone who is seen as representing a barbaric and evil civilization.

Commentators with little or no expertise have jumped into the fray and are feeding into the hysteria. The most nonsensical theories and shabby scholarship pass for serious commentary. It is a tidal wave of ignorance and prejudice against Muslims. Matters are made worse by too few Muslims who can engage in the discussion seriously or on the basis of scholarship. The gaps between Muslims and non-Muslims seem to be widening.

After September 11 there is no greater need than to bridge these gaps of misunderstanding. It is important to convey the basic history of Islam. With this information will come an automatic refutation of the current image of Islam as a barbaric civilization. It is the duty of every scholar and commentator to engage in this exercise. Islam will remain an area of interest for a long time to come. After all, there are 1.3 billion Muslims in the world and 57 states claim to be Muslim. There are some 7 million Muslims in the U.S.

Mark Graham argues that there is a clear connection between Islamic civilization and the European Renaissance and he sets out to detail the impact of the Muslim world on European science, poetry, art, philosophy, mathematics and medicine. Graham did not set out to write a heavy academic tome. This is not a history book with heavily annotated pages and dense footnotes. It is a light but substantial read. He believes that there are far too few books on this topic especially in America and feels the need to present the information in an easily digestible format. He is also aware that in the present cultural climate for an author to assert that Islam as a cultural entity was every bit as modern, secular and civilized as the West, that in fact it taught the West to be the way it is, is controversial. But Graham believes passionately in his subject. His introduction sets the stage for his argument: "This is a story that needs to be told … It is the story of how a precious heritage of knowledge was not simply preserved but reconstituted and re-imagined. And it is the story of how medieval Europe gave birth to the Renaissance. This is the story of how Islam created the modern world."

Graham points out Qur'anic verses which should be well received in America. For example the Qur'anic verse: "The nearest in affection to the Muslims are those who say 'We are Christians'" (The Qur'an, Surah 5: Verse 85).

Or "Say: We believe in that which is revealed to us and which was revealed to you. Our God and your God is one. To Him we surrender ourselves" (Surah 29: Verse 46).

Apart from a brief fast-moving history of early Islam, Graham points to the remarkable Muslim figures who lived a thousand years ago and laid the foundations for a sophisticated Muslim civilization which in turn created the conditions for the birth of the Renaissance.

The key was the translation of the Greeks. It was the Muslim scholars who over the centuries translated the great Greek masters into Arabic and which allowed them to be translated into Latin and eventually into French and English. With the Greeks came ideas of logical thought, political discussion and of good governance, philosophy and ethics.

Yet Graham points out that if you look through the pages of a standard high school text on Western civilization you will be hard pressed to find mention of any Muslim other than the Prophet of Islam. Perhaps the name of Saladin or Suleman the Magnificent but nothing more. That is why Graham has set out to rectify the gap that exists in Western knowledge.

Classical ideals created humanism, rationalism and enlightenment, the basis for Western civilization. Yet paradoxically the Muslims are told that the Greeks belong to Christendom and not Islam. In a powerful ending Graham points out that the Greeks indeed belong to Islam as much as they ever did to Christendom. It was the Muslims who saved the Greeks when the Christians were burning them. It is they who translated them, debated them, commented on them and improved upon their systems. Muslims gave Western Christians their science, medicine, music, food, clothes, poetry, philosophy and mathematics. They were the ones who pulled Europe out of the dark ages and into the enlightenment. "This", Graham believes, "is the terrible secret that the Renaissance myth tries to hide" (p. 182).

Graham's last lines sum up his thesis: "It is time for memory to triumph over collective amnesia. Islam belongs to the West as much as the Egyptians or the Greeks .. It is in the writing of that new history that we might finally unlearn what has pulled us apart and learn anew what we share as children of Abraham and Aristotle" (p. 182).

It is this message of hope and reconciliation that makes Mark Graham's *How Islam Created the Modern World* essential reading. It would be an important—and enjoyable—book to read in normal times; in the post-September 11 world it should be required reading.

Professor Akbar Ahmed
Ibn Khaldun Chair of Islamic Studies
and Professor of International Relations
American University
Washington, D.C.20016

Introduction

This is a story that needs to be told. It is a story that has largely been forgotten, its remnants embalmed in technical journals and texts that only a handful of specialists read. Open any high school history textbook and you will see this story noticeably absent, as you would in most undergraduate world history surveys. It is the story of how a religion many have come to see as barbaric and anti-modern built an empire of wealth and splendor the like of which the world had never seen. It is the story of how a precious heritage of knowledge was not simply preserved but reconstituted and reimagined. And it is the story of how medieval Europe gave birth to the Renaissance.

This is the story of how Islam created the modern world.

1

Islam Becomes
An Empire

THE MESSENGER

We know when it all began: toward the end of the month of Ramadan, around 610 CE. We also know the place: the hills skirting the Arabian trading hub of Mecca. Most of all we know the one who first heard the news: Muhammad, a merchant who often journeyed to the loneliness of a cave in Mount Hira to think and pray.

While meditating in the cave one night, he heard a voice say: "Read!"

The illiterate Muhammad was bewildered by the mysterious command.

"Read!" the voice said again, "in the name of your Lord who created---created man from clots of blood. Read! Your Lord is the Most Bountiful One, who by the pen taught man what he did not know."

As Muhammad made a hasty exit, the voice called back to him, "O, Muhammad, you are the messenger of God, and I am the angel Gabriel."

He ran home so terrified that he cried to his wife Khadija, "Cover me!" But the voice did not go away. Over time, Muhammad was given many more revelations through Gabriel, words straight from Allah Himself, the God of Abraham, Moses and Jesus. Now Muhammad had become the "Seal of the Prophets," the last in that long chain.

Naturally, the citizens of Muhammad's hometown were not especially thrilled to hear his monotheistic message. Mecca owed its prosperity to its shrine, the Ka'ba, where the myriad gods of the various Arab tribes shared space. In this environment of religious inclusiveness, feuds and factions took a backseat to pilgrimage. Mecca had become a highly lucrative caravan stop. The Quraysh, the Arab tribe who controlled the city, had no interest in a religion that made their source of income obsolete.

The new prophet's followers were few at first, mostly recruited, as Jesus' had been, from the less fortunate. To them, the Qur'an's message of justice and mercy to the poor and the outcast was a miracle in itself, emerging in the midst of such brutality and inequality (for a brief sampling of Qur'anic passages, see Appendix I). The callous rich who despised and victimized them were in for a big surprise. Muhammad had found something more powerful than their money or their honor. He had found Allah:

> Confound man! How ungrateful he is.
> From what did He create him?
> From a drop He created him and fixed his destiny,
> Then He laid down his path for him.
> Then caused him to die and laid him in the grave.
> – Qur'an (80:17-21)

Suddenly, human wealth and tribal pride were as nothing. Islam, or submission to God, became the new order of the day. What submission entails is relatively simple:

Your Lord, magnify.
Your garments, purify.
All pollution shun.
Do not fear in giving alms to give too much.
For your Lord, wait patiently.
– Qur'an (74:3-7)

The Meccans at first listened to Muhammad with casual amusement. These harmless, simple pieties were all well and good. But
when the new Prophet began to preach against their idols, they grew
incensed. What angered them the most was Muhammad's declaration
that all idol-worshippers had hellfire as their reward. To the tribal
Meccans this was too much. They began to taunt Muhammad, throwing sheep guts at him as he walked the streets. Eventually the teasing
grew into outright threats. Despite such animosity, his uncle Abu
Talib managed to protect Muhammad long enough for the Prophet to
recruit a band of several hundred converts.

When the universally respected Abu Talib died in 619 Mecca
became even less inviting than before. Khadija, the first convert to
Islam and the one who had supported Muhammad with her love
and kindness, died soon after. The Quraysh began to intensify their
persecution of the Prophet and his followers. Muhammad thought of
moving his community to the summer resort of Ta'if, seventy miles
away. He made an initial journey on his own, hoping to find a city
eager to hear his message. Upon his arrival, however, he was given a
rude reception. Worshipppers of the goddess al-Lat hounded the
Prophet out of town, lobbing rocks and curses all the way.

Demoralized, Muhammad made the long journey back to
Mecca. This time, the Prophet met with a caravan group from
Yathrib, two hundred and fifty miles north. They invited him and
his followers to their town, thinking that he might be the Messiah
their Jewish neighbors were expecting to show up at any moment.

Muhammad accepted their invitation—and not a moment too soon. A hostile Meccan clan decided to stab the Prophet while he slept. When the killers burst into Muhammad's bedroom, however, they found a decoy—Ali, his nephew and ward. The Prophet and his faithful follower, Abu Bakr, had quietly slipped out of Mecca the night before. Furious, the plotters gave chase.

Meanwhile the two fugitives had staked out a cave on Mount Thawr. The Meccans soon reached the mountain and searched it thoroughly. The assassins found the cave where the Prophet lay hidden. Yet they turned away without entering and rode back to their city. What stopped them from skewering the hated Muhammad right there?

As the story goes, as soon as the Prophet stashed himself in the cave, a spider began to weave its web across the entrance. The Meccans, seeing the web, reasoned that no one had run through the mouth of the cave for quite some time. Islam was saved by the slender strand of a spider's web.

From this *hijra*, or emigration to Yathrib (which eventually became known as Medina, the City of the Prophet), the Islamic calendar begins. The date was July 16, 622.

Once safely within the walls of Medina, Muhammad began to shape the Muslims into a highly cohesive, passionately spiritual community, the *umma*. Many Islamic practices were introduced here, including mosques, muezzins, the direction of prayer, and many *surahs*, or chapters, of the Qur'an.

At Medina, Muhammad developed an intense bond with his followers. Like many great figures, his thoughts, deeds, and habits were reverently preserved. We know a great deal about Muhammad from his sayings, the hadith. According to Mahatma Gandhi, these sayings "are among the treasures of mankind, not merely Muslims." The hadith not only express the Prophet's views on faith and social justice but also detail his private life and tastes. One endearing story relates how Muhammad cut away part of his sleeve as he went to prayer. The Prophet, as it turns out, was worried lest he disturb his sleeping cat, Muizza, nestling in his arm.

Muhammad's compassion for not just humans but all creatures is evident in one of his most famous parables (*Hadith of Bukhari* 44:16:538), the story of a prostitute who, walking by a well, saw a dog dying of thirst. Taking off her shoe and tying it with her shawl, she drew some water for the poor animal. For this simple act of kindness, Muhammad told his listeners, God forgave the woman for her licentious life. This parable, akin to Jesus' tale of the Good Samaritan, reflects not only the Prophet's empathy toward social outcasts but also the Qur'an's message of tolerance and mercy.

Muhammad's brilliance lay in politics as well as spirituality. One of the most extraordinary events to take place during this time was the drafting of the Covenant of Medina (*Sahifat al-Madinah*), what some consider to be the world's first constitution. It was a treaty and city charter between the Arabs and Jews of the city. All groups (Muslims, Jews, and non-Muslim Arabs) pledged to live in civic harmony, governed by mutual advice and consultation. The Covenant bound these varied groups into a common defense pact and stipulated that the Jews of the city were one community with the Muslims, that they were free to profess and practice their religion and that they were entitled to all the rights pertaining to the Muslims. This amazingly foresighted document was a revolutionary step forward in civil government. Despite the ultimately tragic end of Muslim and Jewish cooperation in Medina, this blueprint of interreligious tolerance would serve Islam and its subject peoples well in the future.

The resolve of Medina's citizens would soon be tested. After years of tension, the conflict between Muslims and Meccans erupted into open war. The showdown came in March 624. Learning that a large Qurayshite caravan would pass nearby on the way to Mecca, Muhammad decided to meet them and inflict a military and financial defeat.

The raid became known as the Battle of Badr. The Meccans had brought a support of nine hundred and fifty men, most of them mounted, to guard the thousand camels and their treasure, worth 50,000 dinars. Muhammad, on the other hand, could only manage a paltry three hundred or so, some of them old men. The Muslims had only seventy camels and two horses. Clearly they would be annihilated.

The battle began in true Arabian fashion, with single combat between champions from each side. Afterwards the sword slinging erupted in earnest, with the cocky Quraysh assured of victory.

Despite their initial enthusiasm, the Meccans quickly discovered that the Muslims had the advantage of superior organization as well as control of all the nearby wells. The Meccans were now in a fight for water as well as their merchandise. For their part, the Muslims fought courageously, with the unwavering conviction that God was on their side.

By the time the dust had cleared and the blood soaked in the dust, Islam had fourteen martyrs. The Meccans lost seventy men, with seventy more taken prisoner. The forces of the Prophet had won a stunning victory.

Later, it was revealed to the Prophet that Allah had sent a thousand angels to fight with him, lest the all-too mortal Muslims grow arrogant with their success. Meanwhile Allah sent a stern warning to the defeated Quraysh:

Taste this. The scourge of the Fire awaits the unbelievers.
– Qur'an (8.14)

The Quraysh waited a year to settle the score, bringing three thousand men to what would soon be called the Battle of Uhud. Muhammad, meanwhile, had increased his force to seven hundred. The odds did not favor the Muslims, though they soon gained the upper hand, as they had at Badr.

A group of Muslim archers could taste the victory. Even though they were ordered to maintain their position at the top of Mount Uhud, they now dashed headlong into battle. Their recklessness enabled the Meccans to regroup. Within no time, a counter-attack was mounted by the redoubtable Khalid ibn al-Walid and the Muslims were in complete disarray. Muhammad himself took part in the fighting, using both bow and spear. In the ensuing melee, the Prophet was knocked down by a stone, splitting his lip and smashing a tooth. A Quraysh warrior sent him reeling backwards, falling into a hole. After being hauled to safety, the stunned Muhammad quickly recovered. But in the meantime a rumor spread that he had been killed. His demoralized followers fled in panic.

When the battle was over, twenty-two Meccans and sixty-five Muslims were dead. Their fields had been trampled by the invading army and their harvest ruined. And as a gruesome parting shot, the Meccans defaced the Muslim dead, making necklaces of their ears and noses. Hind, the wife of the Quraysh leader Abu Sufyan, tore out the liver of Muhammad's uncle Hamza, chewed it up and spat it out in revenge for the death of her father at Badr. The two parties vowed to meet again in a year.

It actually took a couple years and in the ensuing time Muhammad's popularity was at an all-time low. The divine favor that was theirs at Badr was gone, the Muslims reasoned. If Allah couldn't guarantee victories, why bother listening to his Prophet? In the midst of this discontent, a revelation arrived which assured the faithful that Uhud had been a test of their resolve and a punishment for those who felt they could accomplish anything without God's help.

The Prophet was being assailed from many sides. Just as his own followers were beginning to question him, so too were the Jews of Medina. After many years they had not been persuaded to leave their faith. Nor had they come to accept Muhammad as their Messiah.

The Prophet was bewildered. To him, Islam was simply the final stage in a process that began long ago with Abraham, their mutual father who had built the Ka'ba in the first place. Muhammad had married a Jew.

Muslims celebrated some Jewish holidays and kept the Yom Kippur fast. In spite of this, the Jews rejected the new Prophet as they had another, six hundred years before. It was one of the greatest disappointments of Muhammad's life.

By 627 the Meccans were back with ten thousand men, including Bedouin mercenaries, African slaves and various Jewish tribes; an international coalition, so to speak. It didn't help that Muhammad only had three thousand of the faithful.

The Prophet had learned his lesson at Uhud and decided against engaging them on the open field. Following the advice of a Persian convert, he commanded his followers to dig a trench around the entire city of Medina. It took them twenty days to complete it. The invaders' siege lasted little longer. In a month they withdrew, unable to breach Medina's defenses. Muhammad had scored an almost bloodless victory—only twenty men had died. Now there was nothing to stand in Islam's way.

Not long after the battle of the trench, Muhammad turned on the remaining Jews in Medina, whom he suspected of conspiracy with the Meccans. An Arab tribe, the Aws, pleaded their case, and the Prophet let the Aws chieftain decide their fate. This man, however, proved to be less than sympathetic. He ordered the males beheaded and the women and children sold into slavery. Muhammad, still stung by their rejection of Allah's message, let the punishment stand.

For the next several years, the message of Islam was brought to the other people of the Book, the Christians. As the Qur'an (29:46) puts it:

Say: We believe in that which is revealed to us and which was revealed to you. Our God and your God is one. To Him we surrender ourselves.

And:

The nearest in affection to [the Muslims] are those who say: 'We are Christians.'
– Qur'an (5:85)

Some of the Christians grew so affectionate toward Islam that they converted. One was a Byzantine priest named Dughatir. Another was the prefect of Palestine. Dughatir was hanged while the prefect, by order of the emperor, was decapitated and crucified. Despite these brutal retaliations, numerous treaties were signed with Christian and Jewish tribes.

Other Christians, however, were not so friendly. An expedition of Muslims into Syria was decimated by a Byzantine border patrol that slew, among many others, the Prophet's adopted son. It was the beginning of a less than beautiful friendship that would finally expire in 1453, when Constantinople became Istanbul.

Through treaties, conquests and even assassinations, the Arabian peninsula was quickly brought under the sway of the One God's banner. During this time the Muslims held to strict rules of engagement which forbade harming women, children, animals and even trees. While Muhammad did burn an orchard or two when it was necessary to provoke surrender, his enlightened and civilized approach to combat was a moral milestone.

In 630, Muhammad finally entered Mecca with ten thousand men. Abu Sufyan, the Umayyad chieftain who had opposed him at Badr and Uhud, surrendered. The army of the Prophet occupied Mecca without a fight.

Instead of executing his former archenemies, the Prophet let them go free—even Abu Sufyan's wife Hind, who had cut open the body of Muhammad's uncle and chewed his liver. Her son Mu'awiya became the Prophet's new secretary. It was an almost unprecedented act of peace and a brilliant diplomatic move for Islam, making the conversion of Mecca all the easier.

The Prophet's wrath was reserved solely for the idols within the Ka'ba. Dragging the wooden stumps out into the open, the Muslims smashed them apart one by one and ground them into the dust. All that remained were some paintings of Jesus and the Virgin

Mary, which were respectfully removed. The once pagan shrine was rededicated to the only true God. The call to prayer of Bilal, the first muezzin, could be heard throughout the city.

And yet, some Arabs still held out against the onslaught of Islam. Chief among them were the citizens of Ta'if, the very place where Muhammad was stoned out of town years before. After Yemen, Oman, Bahrain and the rest of the Arabian peninsula had submitted, the citizens of Ta'if remained steadfast to their al-Lat. When Muhammad arrived in town with a considerably larger retinue this time, the pagans offered a compromise—they would submit if Muhammad would keep his hands off their idol for three years.

"Three years!" Muhammad cried. "No, not for one day."

Al-Lat perished with one blow of the axe. Paganism in Arabia was dead, a new faith was born, and the world was never going to be the same.

The Rightly Guided

Muhammad died two years later, on June 8, 632. He was buried under the floor of his favorite wife A'isha's home in Medina. His father-in-law and faithful follower Abu Bakr addressed the faithful:

> O people, truly, whoever worshipped Muhammad know that Muhammad is dead. But whoever worshipped God, know that God is alive.

There would be no other prophets. Allah had given his final revelation. All that was left for the survivors was to spread the news.

But the Muslims were not to be without a leader, though Muhammad had no sons to pick up the mantle. The position first passed to Abu Bakr and then to Umar, the son-in-law of the Prophet. The idea of kingship being anathema to the Arabs, these men were simply called *khalifa* or "successors."

For thirty years, the whole of Islam was ruled by these caliphs who put as much store in spirituality as politics. As Abu Bakr put it: "Obey me as long as I obey God and His Prophet. When I disobey Him or His Prophet, then do not obey me."

During this time, the revelations of Muhammad were often memorized word for word by the faithful. But they were also written down—on papyrus, palm fronds, cloth and even camel bones. In recent years some early versions of the Qur'an have been discovered which contain textual variations. According to most Muslim scholars, this has more to do with Arab dialects than doctrinal differences. Abu Bakr instructed Muhammad's scribe, Zayd bin Thabit, to make a master copy of all the fragments in existence. From him, the first Qur'an was passed down to Umar and finally to Uthman, the third caliph, who compiled the definitive text. Unlike the Jewish and Christian scriptures therefore, the Qur'an was compiled within the lifetimes of those who had first heard its revelations. After reading the Qur'an to the Prophet's companions, who approved it, Uthman had all other copies destroyed.

Some scholars dispute this story, claiming that the Qur'an did not achieve its standard form till a much later date. They call attention to the fact that copies of the Qur'an from this early period are no longer extant. However, they fail to mention that the art of several mosques and shrines such as the Dome of the Rock have preserved Qur'anic verses from this era. In 903 a traveller to the Prophet's mosque described mosaic inscriptions there that included surahs 1 and 91-114. The mosaics were created between 706-710. Thus the evidence indicates that at a very early date the Qur'an existed in canonical form.

Even for the skeptical, the period for possible redaction of the Qur'an was quite brief compared to the Judeo-Christian Bible. Given this evidence it seems likely that the definitive Qur'an of Uthman is the same that is read by every Muslim today.

Besides the compilation of their holy scripture, the leaders of Islam had other pressing affairs at hand. These early caliphs may not have been experienced governors but they did what was necessary to hold the motley array of tribes together under the single banner of Islam. Without the charisma of the prophet to unite them, the Arabs tended to revert to tribal loyalties, feuds and even some pagan practices from the "age of ignorance."

From the moment of the Prophet's death in 632, Islam as a unified political and spiritual entity ceased to exist. Sects and factions sprang up like scorpions. Rivalries were as pandemic as in early Christianity, with its contentious adherents to Peter, Paul, or Apollos. Nothing has changed. In fact, division and schism have multiplied with the centuries.

Today, contrary to the common perception, there is no such thing as "Islam" but many different Islams, as there are many different Judaisms, Christianities, or Buddhisms. Europeans and Americans have made mortal blunders and missed many opportunities for reconciliation over the years because they have failed to understand Islam in all its factional complexity.

This factionalism was the undoing of the first group of caliphs. All relatives of the Prophet, these "Rightly Guided" caliphs attempted to maintain the common sense of purpose and submission to Allah's will that characterized the first community at Medina. Sadly, they failed—martyrs to the faith of Islam and perhaps victims of its political triumphs.

When Umar died, the community nominated both Uthman and Ali. The vote was split but eventually they settled on Uthman. Despite his accomplishments as a ruler, including standardizing the holy book, Uthman made many political enemies, especially in Egypt. After replacing its popular governor with his own cousin, Uthman came under fire from a group of five hundred Arab rebels. First he promised to consider their demands. Then he reneged on his promise and preached against them at a Friday service. Enraged, the rebels broke into his home and killed him while he was reading the Qur'an.

It was not a good way for Ali to gain the caliphate. There were prob-lems from the very beginning. Ai'sha, the Prophet's wife, was no friend of Ali, who angered her years before when she had been accused by her enemies of adultery. At the Battle of the Camel, she led rebel forces against him, urging her troops on while ensconced in a litter on a camel's hump. Ali was victorious that day and forced Muhammad's widow into seclusion. He was not so successful with another, more dangerous rival.

Mu'awiya, the son of Muhammad's former arch-enemy Abu Sufyan, had risen quickly to power in the new Islamic state. He was now the powerful governor of Syria, owing his position to the slain Uthman, a relative. The governor lost no time in accusing Ali of having conspired to kill Islam's rightful ruler. Soon it came to open war.

After the inconclusive Battle of Siffin in 657, Ali decided to leave the matter to arbitration. This was the last straw for a group of Muslims who felt it was sacrilege to submit God's word to diplomacy. Known as the Kharijites, they mustered an army against him a year later. Ali won the battle that day but lost the war. Three years later, while entering a mosque, a Kharijite fanatic leaped from his hiding place and plunged a dagger into the caliph, killing him on the spot.

Ali's followers shifted their loyalties to his son Hasan, but to no avail. Selling out his claim to the caliphate, he retired to Medina while Mu'awiya became the first caliph of the Umayyad dynasty. The unbroken chain of Rightly Guided Caliphs—relatives of the Prophet himself—was broken. After years of bloody civil war, Islam passed from the hands of spiritual guides to worldly monarchs. The death of Ali left a scar that would never be healed, leading to an increasing array of violent schisms that would shake not just Islam but the world.

To the Muslims of today, the reign of the Rightly Guided Caliphs was an era of spiritual purity, akin to the Apostolic Age of Christianity. Perhaps it is all just nostalgia, a yearning for a heroic past that can outshine the lackluster present. But one thing is certain—things were never the same after Mu'awiya became caliph.

With the Umayyads the capital moved from Mecca to Damascus, and Islam lost its political and spiritual focus in Arabia. From here on, the new world power would become increasingly cosmopolitan and multi-ethnic. Islam was about to become an empire.

The Conquests

A year after the Prophet's death, a vast army of Muslim warriors invaded the great Sassanian Empire of Iran. The leader of the faithful, Khalid ibn al-Walid, was not a man to mince words. In a terse letter to the Persians he invited them to either become Muslim or to pay the *jizya*, a tax imposed on non-Muslim subject people. If they chose neither, Khalid assured them that "I shall come against you with men who love death as you love to drink wine."

Nothing could withstand them. Within a century, Muslims had done what Rome could not do: conquer the entire civilized world. The call of the muezzin could be heard from Spain all the way to India. By 732, a hundred years exactly after Muhammad's death, Muslims were skirmishing with Franks at Poitiers.

Khalid ibn al-Walid, the greatest of Muslim warriors, was the leader of the initial conquests in the Near East. Ironically, the Meccan had fought against the Prophet at Uhud, nearly crushing him that day. Now a convert, he shook the two great kingdoms of Byzantium and Sassanian Persia to their foundations and blazed the trail for a new empire, grander than any the world had ever seen.

It was not the first time empires had been prey to marauding invaders. Visigoths, Ostrogoths, and Vandals had sacked Rome. The Huns and Vikings put the dark in Europe's dark ages. But none of these groups left any truly lasting impact on the societies they raped and pillaged. Instead they were quickly absorbed into the Latin Christian culture of Rome, going native almost immediately.

The Muslims were different. They had the revelation of God to back them up, a new faith that outdid all others. Conversion was the order of the day—and not always on the most pleasant of terms. They were not interested in assimilation. Since God's words had been dictated to Muhammad in Arabic, the language itself was holy. Rather than learning Greek or Persian or Latin, the Arabs saw to it that Arabic became *the* world language, the tongue of civilization for the next six hundred years.

Khalid's armies were in the right place at the right time. The two great world empires of Byzantium and Persia were weakened by decades of warfare. As within any empire, their conquered peoples began to slowly erode the shackles of power. Monophysite and Coptic Christians were considered heretics by the orthodox Byzantines. When Khalid besieged Damascus in 635, Arab Christians from within its walls conspired with him against their Orthodox overlords. When the Byzantines were defeated and expelled, the populace greeted the Muslim armies with open arms. Despite their being Christian, the Syrians had more in common with their fellow Arabs than the overbearing Greeks of Constantinople.

A year later, at the Battle of Yarmuk, an eastern tributary of the Jordan, Khalid's forces faced fifty thousand Byzantine troops commanded by the emperor's brother Theodorus. Khalid was able to maneuver the Greeks into a narrow space between two streams. There they were blinded by sand blowing in fitful gusts. The battle cry of "Allahu akbar!" (God is the greatest!), spurred the Muslims on. They slaughtered their opponents, driving them into the stream beds. There were barely any survivors. The Emperor Heraclius mourned, "Farewell O Syria, and what an excellent country this is for the enemy."

Eventually, the caliph Umar grew jealous of Khalid's popularity and success. Summoning him back to Medina, the caliph stripped the great general of his position and left him to die in modest obscurity in 642.

Khalid's legacy would far outlast his fame. Now, nearly fourteen centuries after his death, the Prophet's banner still flies over the lands Khalid and his armies conquered so long ago. While Catholic Christianity, the other great temporal and spiritual power of the age, lost its touch over a great deal of Europe, Islam maintained its hold over its vast domains—a testament to the culture and faith of Muslims worldwide.

THE UMAYYADS

Under Mu'awiya the army's tribal units were broken up and reorganized along a more modern, Byzantine model. Far from the unruly desert warriors that had won Badr, these new Umayyad soldiers were disciplined, well paid, and followed a strict chain of command. When he became governor of Syria, Mu'awiya found shipyards (*dar al-sina'ah*, from which English gets the word *arsenal*) along the Mediterranean coast. Seeing the strategic advantage, he oversaw the construction of Islam's first navy and declared himself the *amir al-bahr*, "commander of the sea." The term he coined would later surface in Europe, where it was changed to *admiral.*

Despite Mu'awiya's bloody rise to power, his reign marked one of the longest periods of internal peace for any caliph. "War costs more," he replied when someone castigated him for his lavish spending.

This did not stop the armies of Islam from taking their message to Byzantium and Northern Africa. During Mu'awiya's reign, Muslim armies besieged Constantinople for nine years. The siege itself was unsuccessful due to a Byzantine concoction known as "Greek fire," a kind of early napalm.

While the capital of the Greeks stood fast, the Byzantine holdings in Northern Africa were falling to Islam, one after the other. First it was Egypt, where the conquerors founded a new city known as Cairo. From there they proceeded into Tunisia until they were finally checked by the native Berbers.

At the death of Mu'awiya, his son Yazid ascended to the throne. It was official now: the Arabs had a king. The political reality did not sit well with many. Yazid was nowhere near the statesman or general that his father had been. His lackluster siege of Byzantium had won him no glory and his love of flesh and wine repulsed those who took Allah at his word. Dissent swelled until a champion was chosen to vanquish Yazid. This was Hussayn, the son of Ali and grandson of Muhammad himself.

Hussayn had lived quietly in Medina, gathering around him a circle of devoted followers who revered him as their imam and future caliph. Now he refused allegiance to Mu'awiya's heir and set off across the Iraqi desert to confront him.

His journey had barely commenced when warning came that the viceroy of Iraq's son, Ubaid Allah, was waiting to crush any uprising that came his way. Once they heard the news, Hussayn's Bedouin soldiers fled back into the desert, leaving him with only seventy men.

The imam shrugged and rode on, expecting a mass revolt when he reached Kufa. But he never had the chance to test his theory. At his camp in Karbala, he was attacked by Ubaid Allah's forces. Refusing to surrender, Hussayn and his men fought them to the death. The overwhelming Umayyad force slaughtered them mercilessly. Hussayn's ten year old nephew died in his arms. His brothers and sons were struck down and finally Hussayn himself fell.

The women and children were spared but the warriors were beheaded. When the head of Hussayn was thrown at the feet of the viceroy someone cried: "Gently—on that face I have seen the lips of the Apostle of God!"

The entire *umma* was horrified by the news. Yazid tried to wash Hussayn's blood from his hands but the memory of the slaughter at Karbala would resonate through the centuries, creating a martyr for a messianic sect of Islam known as Shiaism (for more on the Shias, see Chapter 7). The new sect was quickly embraced by many of the empire's outcasts, including those of non-Arab origin like the Persians. Proud of their great cultural and political heritage, the Persians resented the imperious and unschooled Arabs. Embracing Shiaism they, along with many other disaffected Arabs, united in 747 with a distant relative of Muhammad to overthrow the Umayyads.

The Abbasid Revolution

Abu-al-'Abbas was a descendant of the Prophet's first cousin. Appropriately known as *Al-Saffah*, the bloodshedder, Abu-al-'Abbas rallied the enemies of the Umayyad regime under his black banner. Claiming that the Umayyads were secular usurpers with no spiritual authority, he pledged to refocus the caliphate and Islam itself on the Prophet's original vision.

The *mawali*, or recently converted non-Arabs, were his strongest supporters. Taking the Prophet at his word that all Muslims were brothers, they challenged the Arab system of segregation in mosques and marketplaces. These Persians, Syrians, Berbers and others were forced to pay taxes from which Arabs were exempt. They could not marry Arabs, nor could they serve in the higher echelons of the military, notably the cavalry. This huge underclass vastly outnumbered their Arab masters. Clearly, it was time for a change.

By 749, the would-be ruler made his first move in Iraq. Abu-al-'Abbas was proclaimed caliph in Kufa, where Ali had met his doom. From there he sent a Persian ex-slave, Abu-Muslim al-Khurasani, to stir things up across the border. Al-Khurasani soon amassed an army which drove the Umayyads back into Iraq. A year later, on a tributary of the Tigris River, the last Umayyad caliph, Marwan II and his twelve thousand troops were annihilated. The caliph fled to a church where he was soon found and beheaded. The rest of the Umayyad family fared even worse. The royal tombs in Damascus were broken into and the corpses burned to cinders.

But the most atrocious reprisal was yet to come. An uncle of Abu-al-'Abbas, Abdallah ibn Ali, invited eighty men of the former royal family to a banquet, guaranteeing their safety. In the middle of their meal, they were surrounded and clubbed to death. Leather covers were thrown over them as table cloths and Ibn Ali and his killers feasted on the dead and dying of Mu'awiya's heirs.

The year was 750 and the Abbasids, knee-deep in blood, ascended the throne they would hold for five centuries. Despite such a savage start, it was here, in the new capital of Baghdad, that Arabs and Persians alike began a process of experimentation, invention and discovery that would lead to the European Renaissance and beyond.

2

The House of Wisdom

I t was the Dark Ages. Vikings were marauding the coastlines, trade routes were down, thugs in armor set up a protection racket called feudalism, and the wisdom of the Greeks was lost. Meanwhile on the coast of the North Sea, Irish monks saved civilization by preserving what paltry classical texts they had, waiting for the right moment to disseminate them through the Continent and jump-start the Renaissance.

A little while later, during the Crusades, Europe pulled itself out of the Dark Ages by liberating the Holy Land from the "Saracens." Although they were not ultimately successful, the Crusaders managed to bring back all sorts of wonderful things, fragments of Greek and Roman learning that the Muslims had "preserved" or "incubated," faithfully waiting for the true heirs of Plato and Aristotle to reclaim their lost heritage. Once the Muslims had fulfilled this noble function, they returned to their tents and camels and backward ways while Europe went on to the Renaissance and world domination.

FANTASY VS. REALITY

This is how the tale is still often told in the West, from grade school through college. The rise of Islam is mentioned just long enough to explain why there are so many Muslims in the world. After that, Islam fades from the historical record until the Franks encounter the "Saracens" in the 1090s. The success of the First Crusade is recounted with pride, while later failures are quickly glossed over. With the Renaissance wrapping up the account, one might safely conclude that the Europeans could do what the Muslims could not: turn Greek wisdom into something useful.

This is the story of the Middle Ages, the one that every school kid learns. It is the story of how the glory of Greece and the grandeur of Rome were lost for a time but found again—how Europe wandered in the wilderness for forty years (actually more like six or seven hundred) but eventually redeemed itself by throwing out the superstitious worldview of the Catholic Church and embracing the humanistic ideals of the Greek philosophers. What may come as a surprise to the millions of people of all generations who have been forced to learn this version of events is that it is sheer myth.

After all, what could be more mythological than the idea of a hero (Europe), the son of Gods (Greece and Rome), discovering its birthright (civilization and power), after going through a quest (the Crusades) and fighting various monsters (Muslims) who have been hoarding the treasure (philosophy, science, mathematics) for ages? Read it in Ovid, the Nibelungenlied, or J. R. R. Tolkien. But if you really want your heroic fantasy straight up, all you have to do is read a social studies textbook.

Looking through the pages of a standard high school text on Western civilization (or world cultures or whatever other euphemism), you will be hard pressed to find mention of any Muslim other than Muhammad. Perhaps you will come across the names of Saladin or Suleiman the Magnificent, brilliant rulers who, it is begrudgingly admitted, actually defeated the West from time to time. But after that…nothing. No mention of scientists, writers, artists, philosophers—in short, no reference to anyone or anything that would lead you to believe that the Islamic world ever had any culture worth speaking about.

Truth, unlike myth, is frequently what we do not want to hear. And perhaps the most heretical thing to say is that Europe ever had anything to learn from Islam. But learn it did, sitting at the foot of its Muslim teachers for half a millenium. Far from being incubators or preservers, Muslims were all the things those textbooks deny them being: artists, poets, philosophers, mathematicians, chemists, astronomers, physicists. In short, they were civilized at a time when Europe was wallowing in barbarism. Muslim civilization was the greatest in size and technology that the world had ever seen. And far from existing in a vacuum, it directly impinged on the creation of Europe as a cultural entity and as a scientific and political power. As much as some are loathe to admit it, the Islamic world is the giant on whose shoulders the European Renaissance stood.

The story begins at the dawn of the ninth century.

THE CAROLINGIAN "RENAISSANCE"

If there was a bright spot in the Dark Ages, it was Aachen, located in what is now Germany. This was the imperial capital of the Frankish king Charles the Great, known as Charlemagne. From his tribe, the Franks, the modern nation of France derives its name as well as the first great hero of its culture.

Early on in his reign Charlemagne conquered the pagan Saxons and converted them to Christianity after a brutal thirteen-year campaign. From there he turned to the south of his kingdom, which bordered on another non-Christian power quite unlike barbaric Saxony. This was al-Andalus, the Muslim kingdom in Spain, ruled by descendants of the only Umayyads to escape Abu-al-'Abbas' clutches. Here in exile they had turned a backwater peninsula into a center of learning and culture (see Chapter 5).

Like many of his predecessors, Charlemagne had delusions of grandeur about bringing the Gospel to every corner of Europe and beyond. Fortunately for the Muslims, he never had the chance to

Christianize Cordoba. Most of his time in Spain was spent fighting other Christians. Eventually Charlemagne tired of his missionary efforts and marched back home across the Pyrenees. There his rear guard was cut to pieces by Christian Basques. This humiliating defeat served as the basis for the great medieval epic *La Chanson de Roland.*

When he wasn't involved in any of his sixty military campaigns, Charlemagne devoted some time to a first, tentative stab at cultural rebirth in Aachen. He picked an English cleric, Alcuin, to supervise the effort. The enterprising monk set up a palace school where the Frankish nobility could get their first taste of ancient learning. Scholars were imported from Ireland, Italy and Christian Spain. They soon inspired their pupils with such enthusiasm that Aachen was dubbed "the second Athens" or "the second Rome," depending on one's taste in hyperbole.

Unfortunately there was not much Greek or Roman wisdom to go around. Scientific works from ancient Greece were not available in Latin translations, nor was anyone found who could actually read the Greek originals. What remained was largely Roman history and literature. Thanks to the Carolingians, the writings of Julius Caesar, Tacitus and many others were redeemed from obscurity.

After blowing the dust off Rome's literary legacy, monks set about copying the works and dispersing them. This was a labor-intensive process. After flaying the necessary animal to provide a writing surface, the monks had to carefully transcribe the original, word for word, in the new style of handwriting, Carolingian miniscule. Then the manuscript would be turned over to an illuminator who created exquisite illustrations that gave free rein to his fancy.

Primarily then, the Carolingians were responsible for preserving the world's knowledge of Roman literature and revolutionizing manuscript illumination. Considering the time and place, it was no mean achievement. But was this truly a Renaissance? A rebirth of philosophical and scientific speculation?

A few years ago a book was published with the title, *How the Irish*

Saved Civilization. It was those Irish, purported the author, who held on to Roman texts while Vikings burned libraries on the Continent. After the barbarians settled down, the Irish returned to the welcoming arms of Carolingian monks, spreading good cheer and Roman poetry. Thanks to those diligent men, the West rediscovered its classical heritage. The way was paved for Leonardo and Copernicus.

It's a nice story but, alas, history is not that simple. A few beautifully illuminated manuscripts do not a civilization make. One might ask: once civilization was brought back to the Franks, why didn't they do something with it? Because the simple fact is that Europe remained in a feudal stupor for the next four hundred years. Why then did the Renaissance happen when it did? Why were there no great scientific or mathematical discoveries from Charlemagne's reign until the fifteenth century? Why didn't the Europeans use this vast treasure the Irish and Carolingians had saved for them? The answer is simply that what we have learned about "Western" civilization is pure mythology, designed to cover up an embarrassing history of unfathomable ignorance and superstition.

It is curious how great powers consistently legitimize their authority by linking themselves with someone else's glorious past, claiming direct descent from the very best. In this way Western Europe claims Greece and Rome for its pedigree. The Dark Ages were nothing but a temporary amnesia of this great genealogy, thankfully cured by Irish and Carolingian monks. It is certainly what Westerners would like very much to believe.

Except that it is far from the truth. The light of Greek wisdom, the works of Plato and Aristotle, Archimedes and Hippocrates, did not go out in the Middle Ages. Knowledge did not grind to a stop but proceeded at a feverish pace. The Renaissance was already happening and civilization was in no need of being saved. It was alive and well and Charlemagne knew just exactly where it could be found.

In Baghdad.

CHARLEMAGNE'S ELEPHANT

It was there that he sent a delegation in 797 to establish diplomatic ties with the caliph Harun al-Rashid. Known to the Franks as "Aaron, King of the Persians," Harun was no doubt delighted to receive this party of scruffy barbarians. They would be useful in helping him pester his great foes, Umayyad Spain and Byzantium. The way the Frankish chronicler Einhard tells it, Harun showed his esteem for Charlemagne above all other monarchs by showering him with the most extravagant gifts. In reality, the all-powerful caliph most likely considered them nothing more than a token set of baubles. After a series of exchanges between the two empires, Charlemagne received a treasure chest of Eastern bounty: exotic perfumes, bolts of silk, scimitars of Damascus steel, and a marvelous mechanical clock with twelve horsemen popping out of windows to announce the hour.

Most spectacular of all was the gift brought by an Abbasid embassy to Charlemagne's court in 802. After making their way across the Mediterranean, into Italy and through the Alps, Harun's emissaries found themselves at Aachen where they presented the Holy Roman Emperor with a most incredible and awesome spectacle: an elephant.

Named Abu-al-'Abbas, after the dynasty's founder, this white elephant became the marvel of Aachen. Charlemagne had a special house built for his jumbo-sized status symbol and even took him on a military campaign against the Danes. Sadly while the Danish king perished, so, alas, did Abu.

Charlemagne was not to last much longer. In 814 he died, leaving an empire to be split between his various sons. Soon they were at each others' throats, ushering in a new period of social anarchy and intellectual stagnation. The Carolingian Renaissance was snuffed out like a candle in the wind and the Dark Ages were up and running again.

On the surface the initial contact between "East" and "West" bore little fruit. Many scholars, including Einhard, saw this interaction as a sign of Charlemagne's prestige in even remote places like "the Orient."

Yet despite Einhard's glowing account, ties between the two kingdoms remained superficial for the time being. It was only when the Franks came beating at Jerusalem's door three hundred years later that the Islamic world would take any serious notice of its less cultivated neighbors.

Well before the Crusades began, however, Muslims were in the business of changing the course of European history. Harun al-Rashid's impact on Europe would go far beyond an elephant's carcass and a fancy water clock. His greatest gift to his barbaric neighbors was not a bottle of perfume, or a Damascus sword or a bolt of Chinese silk. It was his son, al-Ma'mun, the man who would chart a course for the Scientific Revolution.

THE AGE OF INFORMATION

It all began in Baghdad in 819. Al-Ma'mun had just vanquished his half brother in a struggle for the throne. While his Arab father was the great caliph, his mother Marajil was a Persian slave girl. Once on the throne, al-Ma'mun built a bridge between the two worlds. Soon the cultural riches of Persia, long dormant beneath the yoke of Arab racism, were allowed to fully flower again. Trade flowed freely, industry boomed, and a new class of neo-Muslim merchants made Baghdad the center of the world. The city itself was, in the words of an ancient chronicler, "covered with parks, gardens, villas and beautiful promenades, and plentifully supplied with rich bazaars, and finely built mosques and baths," as well as "numerous colleges of learning, hospitals, infirmaries for both sexes, and lunatic asylums."

The streets, swept and washed clean, were lined by palaces and mansions furnished in silk, brocade, tapestries and Chinese ornaments. In the harbor, there were Assyrian rafts nestling beside Chinese junks, the water "animated by thousands of gondolas, decked with little flags, dancing like sunbeams on the water." To this great international metropolis India brought its minerals and spices, Central Asia its rubies, China its silk, Africa its ivory and Europe its furs. Even the traffic in slavery was multinational, with Africans, Asians, and Europeans toiling beneath Muslim masters. Centuries later, as Baghdad burned to the ground, a newly-formed nation of these slaves would prove to be the salvation of not only Islam but Western Christendom.

Over all this wealth and splendor al-Ma'mun presided. Unlike so many other rulers, however, al-Ma'mun was not content to wallow in pleasure. His imagination was on fire with a revolution of the mind.

In the early years of his life, he had been ostracized from the halls of power for his Persian heritage. His formative years had been spent with his mother in her own country, with a coterie of subversive tutors. After dabbling in Shiaism, al-Ma'mun found a home with a new and radical school of thinkers known as al-Mutazilah, the Seceders. These bold iconoclasts dared to call the nature of the Qur'an into question. According to them, the holy book was created, not eternal as orthodox Muslims believed. The new-found discipline of logic had demonstrated that if God created everything then he must certainly have created the Qur'an as well.

The Mutazilah also puzzled over Qur'anic passages describing the punishment God would inflict on evildoers. Muslims believed in God's omniscience—that he knew everything that men or women would do since before the beginning of time. But if so, the Mutazilah reasoned, how could God punish them for wrongdoings when he knew what would happen before it happened? Could mortals be held responsible and thrown into hell for something over which they had no power?

It was the old conflict between predestination and free will that had divided Christian theologians for centuries. Not surprisingly it was the Nestorian Christians of Syria who first inspired these Muslim radicals to begin their theological quest. Living as a religious minority, the Christians sought ways to defend their faith. The most powerful weapon they had in their arsenal was known as 'aql—reason.

Hellenism (ancient Greek culture and ideals) had arrived in Syria with Alexander the Great and never departed. Just as France and England were part of the Roman cultural sphere, so too was Syria fully in orbit around the classical civilization of Greece. Among the Syrian Christians, Greek was the intellectual language of choice, much as Latin was in the West. From Alexandria to Antioch, wherever Arab Christians crossed intellectual swords with Arab Muslims, they used Aristotle and Plotinus and a host of others to bulwark their arguments.

But Christianity as a whole had a far from amicable relationship with Greek wisdom. Indeed, it was a Christian mob that torched the priceless library at Alexandria centuries before. And it was a Christian king—Justinian—who closed Plato's academy in 529 and sent its scholars packing to the distant lands of Persia and the school of Jundishapur. These Nestorian exiles, hated by the orthodox Byzantines, were the ones who preserved the learning of Greece and passed it on to their Arab brethren. There was only one problem. The Muslims could not read Greek.

Al-Ma'mun understood the importance of Greek philosophy from the beginning. Which of the critics of the Mutazilah could argue with this strange and wonderful new 'aql—this logic and reason? Which of them could stand against Aristotle's *Poetics* or *Metaphysics*?

The caliph wasted no time. Commandeering his father's library in 830, he renamed it *Bait al-Hikma*, the House of Wisdom. Here the great caliph gathered together a polyglot army of scholars who were charged with two great tasks: find all the works of ancient Greece that could be found and then translate them into Arabic.

Al-Ma'mun appointed a Nestorian Christian, Hunayn ibn Ishaq, to lead the new intellectual center. Ibn Ishaq went as far as Byzantium, to the very court of the emperor there, in his tireless quest for Greek knowledge. For every book he translated, the caliph gave him its weight in gold. As a former medical student at Jundishapur, Ibn Ishaq was primarily interested in translating the works of Galen, the classical world's greatest physician. But he was far more than simply a translator. It was Ibn Ishaq who wrote the world's first textbook on ophthalmology, among numerous other original works.

With its army of ninety scholars, the Bait al-Hikma managed to translate a staggering array of authors. In less than a century, Islamic culture was enriched by the likes of Aristotle, Ptolemy, Plato, Euclid, Galen, Hippocrates, Archimedes and countless others. Suddenly *falsafa* (philosophy) had passed from its Christian stewards into Muslim hands.

Philosophical and scientific inquiry burst out of Baghdad with the energy of a supernova. Muslims took the recently-discovered Greek wisdom and used it to create a scientific revolution in every field known to humans—astronomy, mathematics, geography, philosophy, physics, chemistry, medicine, history, literature, horticulture, music, engineering, navigation. By the end of the ninth century, Islam was the greatest intellectual power the world had ever seen.

The way these ideas were transmitted was also revolutionary. While the Irish were supposedly saving civilization on a handful of animal skins, Muslims were using a material that would not be seen in Europe for three more centuries. The Arabs called it *warraq* but we know it as paper. If the printing press helped start the Reformation, it would have accomplished nothing without the paper that Europeans had learned to make from Muslims.

When a Chinese papermaker was captured near Samarqand in 751, Muslims were quick to see the practical advantages of this amazing invention. By the time Harun al-Rashid sent his elephant to Charlemagne, his court's records were all written on paper, not papyrus or animal skins. Paper was also used for recording numerical figures and even spelling out an amount owed by one party to another. While Europeans were bartering goods at the local fair, Muslims were writing paper checks to trading partners on different continents.

During the period that Irish monks were jealously hoarding their manuscripts, a Baghdad suburb's *Suq al Warraqeen* (Stationer's Market) had more than one hundred shops selling books and paper of many shades and colors. One famous bookshop, that of al-Nakim, contained over a thousand books, all written on paper. This at a time when the greatest monasteries of Europe were lucky to have a few dozen books on parchment. These bookstores were not just stores but cultural centers, much like the beatnik coffee shops of the 1950s. Here philosophers and poets would gather to exchange ideas and bask in the rays of an unparalleled culture.

At these shops, the *warraqeen* (stationers) would copy any book available for a fee. They would also "publish" original works dictated by authors. Before the book was released the author was given the chance to correct any errors. Authors even received royalties from the shops where their works were sold. When the Islamic publishing world was at its zenith, the number of new titles published per year was greater than modern New York's.

Paper found its way to other institutions as well. So great was the thirst for knowledge that vast storehouses of books were made available to the citizens of Baghdad. These public libraries could be found in all the great cities of Islam, though perhaps the greatest of all was the Khazain al-Qusu in Cairo, which contained almost two million manuscripts in forty separate rooms.

Cairo was the home of another intellectual innovation, Al-Azhar, founded in 970. It was the first university in the world. Here eager students would devour the works of falsafa, absorbing the greatest Greek, Persian, Hindu and Islamic authors in all the branches of science. After a time, the falsafa of the universities found disfavor in the orthodox *madrassahs*, or religious colleges. The madrassahs had originally been used by Sunnis to combat the heresy of Shiaism. Now a new religious conflict had begun, as the universities became battlegrounds in the war between pure reason and pure faith.

It was very clear on which side al-Ma'mun stood. By creating the House of Wisdom and supporting its translators and scholars, he created what many consider to be the Golden Age of Islam. What is ironic, especially for Islamic fundamentalists, is that when Islam was at its most important and influential, it was a multicultural, highly secularlized society with a great amount of freedom of expression and thought.

But there were limits to that freedom. While Europe attempted to instill a rigid Catholic fundamentalism through the terroristic Inquisition, al-Ma'mun enforced a very different kind of thought control. Issuing a royal decree, he stated that henceforth all citizens must accept that the Qur'an was created and non-eternal. Rational dialogue had given way to coercion. It has never been an effective way to change peoples' minds, no matter how well-meaning the intention.

It was too much, too soon. A sturdy opposition arose. One of those jailed by the inquisition was Ahmed al-Hanbal, a conservative champion who had hundreds of thousands of followers. Today his teachings are particularly influential in Wahhabism, the dominant Islamic sect in Saudi Arabia.

Despite the conservative backlash, however, the intellectual revolution of al-Ma'mun did not need reinforcement. From the moment Hunayn ibn Ishaq had commenced his work of translation, Muslim scholars had begun reading, discussing and arguing. Once they had thoroughly absorbed the wisdom of the Greeks, they began to use this wisdom in new, startling ways.

This was Islamic civilization at its best—not a backward, antimodern world of fundamentalists but a vibrant intellectual culture that was neither xenophobic nor anti-rational. Rather, it embraced everything we call modern and enlightened—science, reason, education, even an early form of multiculturalism. That it condoned other unenlightened practices like human slavery does not disqualify its cultural accomplishments. If it did, we would have to write off not just Greece and Rome but Great Britain and the United States as well.

During the reign of al-Ma'mun, Islam saved Greek civilization. But it did more than that, for the Muslims used the gifts of the Greeks to make new creations and inventions. It was precisely these inventions, in all branches of the arts and sciences, that made possible all the great discoveries that would follow.

3

Hippocrates
Wears A Turban

In medieval Europe, whatever medical knowledge had survived from the Roman era was largely forgotten. Hospitals as we conceive of them did not exist. If you had money you could hire the services of a barber-surgeon and his bottle of leeches. If you were hopeless and homeless, you wound up in a monastery, nursed by well-meaning monks. Some monasteries devoted themselves to caring for victims of specific incurable diseases like St. Anthony's fire, leprosy or blindness.

Caring, however, did not mean curing. The compassionate monks were merely nurses of the divine Doctor. Their primary duty, as always, was to pray for others, imploring God to grant them better health. Surgery, banned by the church in the seventh century, was not even an option. Most often the monastic "hospitals" were convenient places for indigent people to die in relative dignity and comfort.

Things might have been different if Christian monarchs had continued their support of Greek and Roman learning. But two events within one hundred years of each other effectively doomed Europe to medical ignorance for half a millenium. The first was the closing of Edessa's school of Hippocratic medicine in 489 by the Byzantine emperor Zeno. Next came the Academy of Athens, founded by Plato himself. Its faculty of Neoplatonists was devoted to a mystical and philosophical search for truth that challenged church doctrine. This was a threat to orthodoxy that could not be tolerated. The Emperor Justinian closed the Academy in 529.

With the champions of Christendom effectively putting an end to learning in the West, scholars headed for the only other great empire available: Sassanian Persia. Here, at Jundishapur, Nestorian Christian doctors and Neoplatonist philosophers laid the foundation for the Islamic revolution in medicine.

Contrary to popular conception, Greek learning was not "lost" by the Europeans. It was deliberately exiled due to religious fundamentalism. And, not too surprisingly, it was heartily welcomed by Muslims. For the next two hundred years, the Islamic world sat at the feet of Plato's last disciples. By the time Hunayn ibn Ishaq's translations of Galen were completed, Muslims had made Greek and Roman medicine their own.

With this influx of classical learning, Muslims brought on a medical revolution. Before Islam's advent, Persians had made no great strides in advancing Hippocrates' and Galen's art. Only now, with the admixture of Arab faith and Persian culture, did medicine become more than an art and instead transform itself into a science.

THE FIRST HOSPITALS AND PHARMACIES

If we conceive a hospital to be a center for the treatment and cure of disease in a comfortable, clean environment then we owe this concept to Muslims. It was in Baghdad that Harun al-Rashid founded the first modern-style hospital, or *bimaristan*. The year was 805.

The bimaristan was a quite different place from the monastic sick wards of Europe. Patients did not crawl there out of desperation, hoping for nothing more than the last rites and a decent burial. They expected state of the art treatment—not from God but from a qualified physician. And, even more unreasonable by European standards, they expected to get better.

Pharmacology was a highly developed science in the Islamic world. The first official pharmacy opened in Baghdad in the ninth century. By the reign of al-Ma'mun, pharmacists were highly-trained professionals, examined, licensed and inspected by the state. Arab apothecaries introduced countless medicines to the international market, including nutmeg, rhubarb, mercury and sandalwood. The thirteenth century *Corpus of Simples,* by Ibn al-Baitar lists more than one thousand four hundred different drugs, three hundred of which had never been used before.

Unlike some modern nations, the world of Islam employed hemp, understanding its beneficial properties. Muslims also learned to tinge their concoctions with fruit-flavored water—spoonfuls of sugar to make the medicine go down. Pretty soon the rest of the world was sampling these syrups and juleps, both originally Arabic words.

Islamic pharmaceuticals even had an effect on European art history. The drug trade between Islam and Christendom made Italian seafaring republics like Venice fabulously wealthy. As the drugs they brought to Europe began to spread so too did interest in their packaging. Medicine was shipped largely in majolica jars called *albarelli.* These cylindrical jars were designed to preserve thick liquids—especially fruit preserves which were used extensively as herbal medicines. The jars were pinched in the center and around the top and bottom where artisans painted fanciful designs of fruits. For anyone who appreciates Italian faience ware, the history of the art form began in the Islamic pharmacy.

A bimaristan was not just a place to prescribe medicine and heal the sick, however. It was an educational center, where the general public could go to improve their knowledge of health and hygiene and where medical students could cut their teeth on clinical lectures. Each hospital was staffed by a director responsible for giving daily classes, while the day-to-day administration of various wards was handled by a legion of assistants.

Like all medical universities, Islamic hospitals kept extensive libraries. Baghdad, Damascus and Cairo had the greatest medical libraries in the world. Not to be outdone, the Caliph al-Hakam II of al-Andalus founded a library in 960 with thousands of volumes on paper that other Europeans would not use for another three centuries. Paper was not just used for transcribing texts. It was also employed for that time-honored seal of approval: the diploma, issued only after the Abbasid pre-meds had passed their state-approved examinations.

The hospitals themselves were the epitome of comfort and efficiency. There were special wards for wounded patients, those with cataracts and other eye diseases, and fever victims. Men and women were separated with Islamic decorum and female nurses were employed as well as *female* physicians. And lest any modern convenience be left out, these hospitals were air-conditioned by fountains of crystalline water.

Meanwhile in Europe, a man with a stomach ulcer was praying to a patron saint, hoping to make it through the night.

AL-RAZI

For the first thirty years of his life, Abu Bakr al-Razi devoted himself to a wide variety of intellectual pursuits: alchemy, mathematics, philosophy, physics, astronomy. His omnivorous mind explored every philosophical and scientific discipline known to the Islamic world. Then, while staying in Baghdad, he visited its hospital, witnessing the sick and wounded. Horrified by their pain and anguish, al-Razi experienced a conversion. His interests in the cosmological sciences were suddenly eclipsed by an insistent need to end human suffering.

Many decades later, in 918, al-Razi was appointed director of the Baghdad hospital where he had first pledged to study medicine. By that time, he was already known as the greatest physician the world had ever seen.

Born in Iran around 854, al-Razi went to study at the university in Jundishapur, where he devoured the wisdom of three cultures: Persian, Greek and Hindu. Like all scholars of the time, he was fluent in all the arts and sciences, a Renaissance man before the term was invented. After medicine, his greatest passion was *al-kimiya*, the progenitor of modern chemistry, from which that science takes its name. A mixture of metallurgy and mysticism, alchemy sought to transform base metals into gold. But it was also concerned with spiritual transmutation as well, often bypassing scientific inquiry for occult speculation.

Al-Razi, however, had no use for the mystical. He was a die-hard materialist, whose philosophical writings sometimes railed against Qur'anic prophecy and revelation. One of his books, the lost *Tricks of the Prophets*, insisted that there were no such things as miracles and that all the prophets were charlatans. Religion, he claimed, was harmful because it engendered fanaticism, provoked warfare and enforced an unnatural hierarchy over mankind.

A radical even by this era's standards, al-Razi believed that people were created equal and had the natural reason to institute a perfect society without religion. Thus, for him, the cultivation of philosophy was more important than religion and Hippocrates and Euclid had more worth listening to than Muhammad or Jesus. An atomist, al-Razi believed that the universe was composed of invisible particles that were eternal—an idea that was antithetical to what the Qur'an (and the Bible) taught. From these atoms, he claimed, came the basic elements which gave birth to life. In his devotion to the scientific over the theological, al-Razi was precociously modern.

Even fellow scientists and philosophers did not escape his scrutiny. Their ideas, he believed, should be challenged along with the others. Though some considered Aristotle the last word on science in all its branches, al-Razi felt free to critique the great philospher when what he observed did not match Aristotelian theory. Similarly, the writings of Galen were suspect whenever they contradicted observable data.

Thus al-Razi's alchemy lost its mystical tenor and became the modern science of chemistry. By stripping his chemical experiments of any symbolic content, al-Razi became an empirical scientist before the Scientific Revolution existed. And unlike the Greeks, he was less interested in theory than in observation—a hallmark of modern science. Nowhere is this more apparent than in his revolutionary approach to medicine.

During his stay in Baghdad, al-Razi was asked to choose a site for a new hospital. Residents were perplexed to see him hanging up scraps of meat in various locations. Over several days he observed the putrefaction of the meat, finally selecting the area where the scraps had rotted the least. Al-Razi based his knowledge on experiments like these, not on the writings of ancient authorities.

His remarkable, systematic analysis of clinical data helped al-Razi to create a masterpiece of medical literature: *al Judari w-al-Hasbah*. After its first translation into Latin, his treatise was reprinted 40 times from 1498 to 1866, with numerous other translations in modern languages including English in 1848. It was an authority in medical universities well into the eighteenth century, nearly a thousand years after it was written. *Al Judari w-al-Hasbah* was the first accurate clinical study of infectious diseases. In it al-Razi makes a distinction, never made before, between smallpox and measles, details the symptoms of each, and prescribes treatment, even down to the prevention of scars. Cosmetic issues were as important to him as therapeutic ones.

This is because al-Razi understood the power of psychology to effect treatment. Once while treating a prostrated amir, al-Razi placed him naked in a bath and then stood on the poolside insulting him. It did not take long for the formerly prostrated amir to rise from the waters, threatening to kill him. Al-Razi made a hasty exit and when the amir's head had cleared he realized that the taunts had jolted him back to health. The overjoyed amir sent the physician a hearty sum of two thousand dinars in gold and "two hundred ass-loads of corn."

In his *Spiritual Physick*, al-Razi discussed these ailments of the soul and mind. In the fourteenth chapter, "Of Drunkenness," he gives us what could be the first clinical description of the effects of alcoholism. Moving beyond the mere physical, he details the psychological debilitation that ensues:

> ...the constant and assiduous indulgence of pleasure diminishes our enjoyment thereof, reducing that to the position of something necessary for the maintenance of life.

It is as valid a description of addiction today as it was then.

The great physician ministered to the stomach as well as the head. Al-Razi was one of the first to recommend a healthy diet and stress it above and beyond the use of drugs. Bathing went hand in hand with good nutrition—not a difficult prescription for Muslims whose religion demanded cleanliness. For Europeans, on the other hand, the idea of bathing was largely anathema, and would not become popular until the Renaissance, when Islamic attitudes had firmly penetrated its society.

Although surgical knowledge was limited in Islam due to Quranic prohibitions, al-Razi managed to invent new ways to stitch up wounds, including the use of animal guts as sutures. Some of his other innovations include the first descriptions of the recurrent laryngeal nerve and of spina ventosa (an affliction of the bones in tuberculosis victims), as well as the realization that the swelling caused by worms was due to a parasite. He is credited by some with the first use of alcohol as an antiseptic and mercury as a purgative, which medieval Europeans called "Album Rhasis" in his honor. His seminal writings on the diseases of children made al-Razi the father of pediatrics.

Yet beyond all of his amazing inventions, observations and discoveries, it was primarily his literary output that established al-Razi's reputation in Europe for century upon century. The author of two hundred works, al-Razi made his greatest contribution to European medicine with his *al-Hawi*, The Comprehensive Book. Under its Latin title, *Liber Continens,* al-Razi's book became a standard text as soon as it was translated in 1279 by Jewish physicians in the Norman kingdom of Sicily. It was required reading in European medical schools for the next five hundred years. Throughout the fourteenth century, the faculty of Paris owned only nine books. One of them was the Continens. It was considered so valuable that when King Louis XI asked to borrow the book in 1371 the faculty forced him to pay a substantial deposit!

Al-Hawi was the most voluminous work ever written in Arabic, representing the entire sum of medical wisdom. It drew on (for starters) the writings of Hippocrates and Galen, Paul of Aegina, the Byzantine Theodoceus, Aaron the Priest, Masarjawaihi, Thabit ibn Qurra, Susruta the Hindu and Ali al-Tabari, al-Razi's teacher. A compendium of Greek, Persian, and Hindu medicine, *al-Hawi* also contains al-Razi's accounts of his experiments and observations, including aphorisms that became famous in Europe:

> The truth in medicine is a goal that one cannot attain, and everything that is written in books is worth much less than the experience of a physician who reflects and reasons.

In this pivotal statement, blind faith in ancient authorities is rejected for a new empiricism of observation and experimentation. Here, with al-Razi, the scientific humanism that would forever alter European society was born.

Even in old age, he went against the grain. It is said that at the end of his life, al-Razi sold all of his possessions and gave the money to his poorest patients. He died in obscurity and poverty. But on the other side of the world, at the medical school of the University of Paris, there is a face carved in stone at the entranceway. It is the likeness of Rhazes, the Latin name of this greatest of physicians, appropriately placed at the doorway to modern medicine.

Ibn Sina

His name was Abu Ali al-Hussayn ibn 'Abd Allah ibn Sina. To the West he was known as Avicenna. "The prince of physicians," Ibn Sina was the greatest thinker of his age and the author of the most influential medical textbook ever written.

Born in Bukhara in 980, Ibn Sina began his intellectual life at an early age. After learning arithmetic from his grocer, he latched onto whatever wandering scholar came through town, soaking up all the knowledge they possessed. When he was ten he recited the entire Qur'an from memory. In his late teens he read Aristotle's *Metaphysics* forty times, until he had every word of that great work memorized. Gaining access to the Sultan of Bukhara's library, Ibn Sina read works by ancient authors that no one had even heard of. By the age of eighteen, the boy genius mastered medicine, which he called "not one of the difficult sciences."

Four years later his father died and Ibn Sina began his career as a lecturer in astronomy and logic at Jorjur. His interest in astronomy led him to write *Salaman wa-Absal,* what is most likely the first bona fide science fiction story. In this tale, preserved in a commentary by al-Tusi (see chapter 4), the hero journeys to the moon and stars and encounters a host of alien civilizations.

Ibn Sina's writing was not confined to speculative fantasy. During his tenure at Jorjur, he began writing the superlative *al-Qanun fi al-Tibb,* The Canon of Medicine. Like al-Razi's *al-Hawi,* the Canon aimed at summing up all existing medical knowledge. But whereas al-Razi's book displayed his clinical genius, the Canon was marked by a more lucid writing style and organization.

Ibn Sina did not think too highly of al-Razi, saying he should have stuck to "testing stools and urines." Unlike his predecessor, Ibn Sina was no great clinician. Nor was he interested in challenging the theories of Galen and Hippocrates. The absolute truth of doctrine, whether in medicine or theology, was more comfortable than a truth based on individual observation and experimentation. The underpinnings of al-Razi's medicine were especially too radical in the Western world, still in the throes of superstition and ignorance. And so Ibn Sina's Canon became the standard medical textbook in Europe until the sixteenth century and read in some parts of the world until the 1800s.

The Canon is divided into a total of five volumes. The first two concern physiology and hygiene, the third and fourth the treatment of various diseases and the fifth materia medica and pharmacology. It was his fifth volume on drugs that was of special importance to the emerging European medical profession. Cataloguing seven hundred and sixty drugs, some described for the first time, Ibn Sina suggested that any new medicines be tested on animals and humans to assure efficacy and determine any harmful side effects.

Despite his unwavering loyalty to Greek authorities, Ibn Sina had his own wealth of clinical data. The purpose of acquiring such information was obvious to him:

The knowledge of anything, since all things have causes, is not acquired or complete unless it is known by its causes. Therefore in medicine we ought to know the causes of sickness and health. And because health and sickness and their causes are sometimes manifest, and sometimes hidden and not to be comprehended except by the study of symptoms, we must also study the symptoms of health and disease.

The message is clear: slavish reliance on ancient authorities is no longer acceptable. The scientific worldview has arrived. While believing wholeheartedly in the Greek idea of humors—that an imbalance in four bodily fluids was the primary cause of illness—Ibn Sina also theorized that contaminated food, water, and "traces" left in the air by sick people could also lead to infection. He understood the function of the tear ducts and the diagnostic significance of the dilation and contraction of the pupil. Ibn Sina also made note of the fact that during the spread of plague, rats and mice suddenly emerged from their burrows to die in great numbers. It's a detail that might have helped a lot of people a few hundred years later, in 1348.

The Canon was first translated by Gerard of Cremona and went into thirty Latin editions after the church gave its official approval. From the twelfth to the seventeenth centuries, the Canon was the medical authority in all of Christian Europe.

Oddly enough, the adage "physician, heal thyself" applies to no one better than Ibn Sina. A notorious party animal, Ibn Sina dictated a great deal of the Canon to his students during all-night drinking bouts at the local brothel. When he was having a bad case of writer's block, Ibn Sina resorted to the bottle: "At night, when weak or sleepy, I strengthened myself with a glass of wine." That the Qur'an prohibited alcohol did not bother him a bit.

In 1037, at the age of 57, his whoring and drinking caught up with him. Some slaves of his, seeing he was sick, dosed him with opium and fled with his money. Soon afterward he collapsed, his body destroyed by alcoholism.

Ibn Sina's cantakerous and boastful personality was a far cry from the intellectual, noble al-Razi. Yet between the two of them, they made medicine the greatest gift of Islam to the Western world.

A PECULIAR PORTRAIT OF HIPPOCRATES

In the late fourteenth century, Roland of Parma published his *Surgery*. It documents the growing awareness of medical science in southern Italy. What is most remarkable about the tome, however, is not its text, but one of its numerous detailed illustrations.

This particular page shows a variety of procedures: the examination of urine, preparation of instruments, cauterization and so forth. In some of the panels, it is Hippocrates himself, the Greek father of medicine, who is shown at work. How did the Italian Christian artist choose to portray Hippocrates, that greatest of "Western" physicians, the one whose oath doctors still take?

In Arab dress, with a turban.

4

The Great Work

Science, like anything else in European history, only becomes significant when Europeans start doing it. Otherwise, it might as well not exist. To bring it up prematurely would disclose the embarrassing fact that Europeans knew little about science that Muslims did not teach them.

In the Middle Ages, monks frequently had to recycle animal skins when they wrote things down. After wiping the ink off, a trace of the old writing often remained. This is called a palimpsest. In the history of Western science, the palimpsest of Islam is most recognizable. It lingers in the name of our numerals and the stars in our sky. Even in most histories of science, Muslims are begrudgingly given their due.

These Persian and Arab scholars were quick to appreciate the practical uses of the Greek wisdom they inherited. But they did far more than slavishly copy and preserve these texts. By incorporating traditions from India and Persia, they forged a new tradition that laid the foundations of modern science. From magnifying glasses to spherical geometry, from pendulums to insane asylums, the innovations of Islamic science are truly astounding. Perhaps most important of all was the man who taught us how to count.

Al-Khwarizmi

Throughout the Middle Ages, Europe used Roman numerals. Like the Greeks before them, Romans based their numerical system on letters. It was a relatively small stock of symbols, seven in total: I, V, X, L, C, D, M, representing 1, 5, 10, 50, 100, 500 and 1000. Despite its simplicity, some problems remained. Writing out larger numbers could be cumbersome. For example, 1938 is MCMXXXVI-II. In multiplication it was even worse: 57 X 38 = 2166 becomes LVII by XXXVIII = MMCLXVI. This unwieldy system made calculation of large numbers a tedious and time-consuming affair. Arithmetic was largely left to a few specialists who had plenty of time on their hands.

That was until Muhammad ibn Musa al-Khwarizmi joined the House of Wisdom in the early ninth century. A great astronomer who also created an early table cataloguing the latitude and longitude of over 2,000 cities, al-Khwarizmi is primarily known today as one of the most influential mathetmaticians of all time. His seminal book *Calculation of Integration and Equation* changed mathematics forever.

If you're wondering how, a clue is in the Arabic title: *Hisab al-Jabr w-al-Muqabalah.* Look closely and you'll notice an English word hiding in there.

Al-jabr—or in English, algebra.

Al-Khwarizmi may not have invented algebra in the modern sense. The credit goes to the Hindus for first practicing this mathematical art. But it was al-Khwarizmi who introduced algebra to the West. His style was so clear and authoritative that his volume became the standard mathematical text in Europe for four hundred years.

When the book was translated into Latin three hundred years later as *Liber Algorismi*, it made al-Khwarizmi's Latinized name a household word synonymous with arithmetic itself. Our English word "algorithm" is a tribute to this greatest of Muslim mathematicians.

Al-Khwarizmi was dazzled by Hindu mathematics. Seeing the vast potential of its numeric and decimal systems, he wrote several works that introduced Hindu math to Islam. The numbers were so easy to use that they soon became the standard throughout the Muslim world. With the publication of his *Liber Algorismi* in Europe these Hindu numerals became known as Arabic numerals, a gift of the Islamic world to Christendom.

The most astounding number the Arabs showed them was not a number at all, but the lack of one: zero. Muslim mathematicians represented this lack of number by a dot or small circle. They called it *sifr*, an empty object. This word was the source of the English "zero" as well as "cipher." *Sifr* solved a lot of problems in mathematics. It allowed for the expression of difference between two equal quantities as well as positional notation, where the digit's position has a value itself which, combining with the value of the digit, creates the number's value. It was a bold new step in abstraction that led to the higher mathematics of the Renaissance.

The Mathematical Jewel

The first major contribution of Muslim science was the development of the astrolabe. Drawing on information from Greek sources, Muslim astronomers perfected what would become the premier navigational tool for the next seven centuries.

Called the "mathematical jewel" by Muslims, an astrolabe was a metal star-map, measuring the altitude of sun, moon and stars. The end result was a stunningly efficient clock as well as a global positioning device, calculating latitude with great precision. Most Muslim astronomers understood that the earth was anything but flat, agreeing that it was spherical in shape. By defining a terrestrial degree, the astrolabe was able to help astronomers calculate the circumference and diameter of the earth itself. The astrolabe soon proved itself an indispensable tool in astronomy, navigation and surveying.

Europe found out about the astrolabe over a hundred years later. While studying in Muslim Cordoba, the monk Gerbert (who would later become Pope Sylvester II), was the first to discover the gold mine that was Muslim science. After returning to Christendom, he wrote *The Book of the Astrolabe* and made the mathematical jewel intellectually chic. For the next few hundred years, the astrolabe became the technological icon for modern science. At least forty or fifty works on the astrolabe appeared before the end of the sixteenth century. Peter Abelard, a prominent intellectual, even named his son Astrolabe in 1118. It was still trendy two hundred years later when Geoffrey Chaucer, author of the *Canterbury Tales*, wrote his *Treatise on the Astrolabe*. Even as late as 1492, while Columbus was sailing the ocean blue, one of his sailors used an astrolabe to chart their decidedly momentous course.

Astronomy from A(lmagest) to Z(ij)

Medieval Muslims, like any people of any time, were fascinated by the stars. Living in the fertile crescent, they had inherited the land where astronomy was born. Their religion, which commanded them to face Mecca during prayer, stimulated an already fervent interest in the heavens. Muslims were traders and used the stars to guide their caravans and ships safely across desert wastes and stormy seas. Astronomy was not just an intellectual diversion, it was an economic necessity.

A rebirth of astronomy began with the construction of the observatory in 830 at the House of Wisdom. Soon translators had completed an Arabic version of something they called "The Great Work" or *Al-Majisti*, by the greatest of Greek astronomers, Ptolemy. When the West received it hundreds of years later, they would know this Greek book by its Arabic name, *Almagest*.

The *Almagest* was the Bible of astronomy. It held the most accurate descriptions (at the time) of stellar movement. From the time of his writings to the age of Copernicus, Ptolemy's system of the heavens was accepted as gospel. According to him, the earth was at the center of the universe, with all the heavenly bodies revolving around it. There was little differentiation between moons, planets or stars except in name. They were simply heavenly bodies, some closer or further from the earth at various parts of the year. Obviously ignorant of the vacuum that lay in outer space, Ptolemy conceived of the heavenly bodies as attached to eight giant spheres which spun around the fixed Earth. While Ptolemy's theory itself may seem a little *eccentric* today, it was a major step up from believing that the stars were gods. Muslims pounced on Ptolemy's work and soon began writing commentaries which incorporated their own observations.

Concurrent with the discovery of Ptolemy was the arrival of the *siddhanta*, astronomical charts brought to Baghdad by roving Hindu scholars. Combining Greek with Hindu wisdom, Muslims began to create their own astronomy, compiling *zij*, or tables of future stellar and planetary movements. Supremely practical, the Muslims were not as interested in critiquing Ptolemy's system as they were in perfecting workable charts for merchants to use in calculating distance, position and time. From these zij the West derived its concept of beginning the day at midnight rather than noon.

This is not to say that Muslim scholars neglected astronomical theory. In fact they were not long in exposing the holes in the *Almagest*. Abu Abdallah al-Battani pointed out Ptolemy's errors in describing planetary motion. Unlike the Greek, he insisted on the possibility of annular eclipses, where a portion of the sun is visible surrounding the moon. He also demonstrated that the solar apogee (the point in space where the sun seems farthest away from the earth) was not fixed, as Ptolemy had surmised. This led to the discovery of the solar apsides, those points in the earth's orbit when it is closest and farthest from the sun.

Al-Battani's writings on the movement of the stars, planets, moon and sun were so valuable that he was quoted six hundred years later by no less than Copernicus and Galileo. The Latin translation of his major writings *De scientia stellarum* was a must-read for European astronomers into the Renaissance and his treatise on solar and lunar eclipses was used as late as the eighteenth century in the study of lunar motion.

His fellow astronomers made other important and startling discoveries. Omar Khayyam, most famous in the West for writing the metaphysical *Rubaiyyat*, was also the first mathematician to solve equations with cubic roots and an astronomer who accurately calculated the length of a solar year to the sixth decimal (365.242198 days). Al-Biruni's figure on the circumference of the earth was off by only fifty miles. He discussed the rotation of the earth on its axis centuries before Europeans did, measured the specific gravity of certain metals correct to the third decimal place, and also wrote a history of India and designed a mechanical calendar.

COPERNICUS & MUSLIM ASTRONOMERS

The way most histories of Europe would have it, modern science began with Copernicus and Galileo. These two men changed the way Europe looked at the universe. Drawing on what is usually referred to as "rediscovered Greek scholarship" Copernicus, a Polish clergyman, decided that the earth was not stationary but moved around the sun. Galileo backed his theories up so persuasively that he came in conflict with the Catholic Church, which held as doctrine the older Ptolemaic view of the cosmos. Science began its struggle with faith in earnest and soon won out. Progress had triumphed over superstition! The Copernican Revolution, as it is often called, was just one of the many miracles that the revival of Greek and Roman learning made possible.

But was that really all it took—the rediscovery of Greek and Roman learning? It almost seems like something out of mythology again: the young Theseus, unaware of his parentage, lifting the rock to discover the sword, shield and sandals of his father. Once reunited with his lineage, Theseus is ready to fight the forces of evil and bring light to the darkness. Similarly, once Copernicus had rediscovered his scientific lineage in the works of the Greeks, Western science could reactivate itself and give birth to the Enlightenment.

The only problem with this story is that it leaves a certain member of the family tree out of the picture.

His name is Nasir al-Din al-Tusi (1201-1274). Perhaps the most influential medieval astronomer, al-Tusi worked at first for the Assassins at Alamut. When they were conquered by the Mongols, al-Tusi abruptly switched sides. He convinced his new employers to fund the construction of the Maragha observatory (now in Azerbaijan), the first modern scientific research institute with an international staff of astronomers, a professional librarian to oversee a voluminous collection, and a host of (for then) high-tech instruments. Al-Tusi was a true polymath, gifted in philosophy, theology, mathematics and science, and responsible for reviving the work of Ibn Sina in the Islamic world. To understand his part in the Copernican Revolution we must first look at something called the equant problem.

Ptolemy's system was the best explanation at the time for what was going on up there in the heavens. Like the Greeks who came before him, he reasoned that the universe operated under certain rational rules—simple, beautiful and perfect. But for his predecessors, any observed deviation from these supposed rules was ignored—since it was unthinkable that the universe was complex, imperfect or even worse, irrational.

Ptolemy, however, was not one to ignore discrepancies like the irregular orbits of the planets, or the fact that autumn and winter lasted fewer days than spring and summer. If the heavenly spheres rolled about like wheels of a vast machine, how to explain the irregularity?

This is what he came up with: planets revolved in small circles called *epicycles*. These epicycles in turn revolved around certain points on a larger circle surrounding the earth called a *deferent*. Sometimes, however, planets could revolve around a point outside the deferent, on a circle called an *eccentric*. And if these didn't explain its movement, the planet could revolve around an *equant*, the theoretical point in the universe from which truly uniform motion could be seen. But that meant the earth was not quite at the center of the universe anymore. Whoops.

Centuries later, medieval Muslim astronomers could see that the equant solution was nothing of the kind. So how to explain the vagaries of planetary motion? It only took Western civilization about a thousand years to figure it out. After careful thought, Copernicus decided on a new center: the sun.

What is interesting is that Copernicus was not the first to postulate a heliocentric (sun-centered) universe. Some Greek astronomers had already claimed that the sun was the center but couldn't come up with the mathematics to back up their theories. Copernicus was able to support his thesis largely based on the refinements in astronomical mathematics that had taken place in the centuries subsequent to Ptolemy.

Which brings us back to al-Tusi. If you listen to the usual histories of the Copernican Revolution, they credit the rediscovery of Greek wisdom with helping Nicolaus on his way to immortal fame. But to revolutionize astronomy, Copernicus used some mathematical theorems that were unknown to the ancient Greeks. One of them, invented by al-Tusi three hundred years before, explained how circular motion can generate linear motion:

> If one circle rolls inside the circumference of another with radius
> twice as great, then any point on the first describes a straight line
> (a diameter of the fixed circle).

It was this theorem that explained mathematically how orbits which appeared irregular (and thus had to be explained with complicated equants, eccentrics and deferents) were in fact uniform about an axis that passed through their center. And the heart of that axis, as it turned out, was the sun itself. Without the theorem that became known as the *al-Tusi couple*, Copernicus could not have rewritten astronomy.

Dick Teresi has written about the recent discovery of a manuscript in Arabic dated before 1350 which preserves al-Tusi's work. Strangely enough, he points out, the geometric symbols al-Tusi uses are identical to those Copernicus employs when discussing the same theorem.

In the early sixteenth century the Italian city of Padua was a

knowledge center, making available not only Arabic works in transla-
tion but original manuscripts as well. It just so happens that Nicolaus
Copernicus studied in Padua, at precisely the time when certain
Arabic astronomical texts were first being made available in Europe.

At the same time, it seems possible that Copernicus was familiar-
izing himself with the writings of another Muslim astronomer, Ibn
al-Shatir (1304-1375). A native of Damascus, al-Shatir was the author
of a book called *A Final Inquiry Concerning the Rectification of
Planetary Theory*, wherein he rid the Ptolemaic system of cumbersome
equants and, in his words, created "universal models for the planetary
motions in longitude and latitude and all other observable features of
their motions." While still adhering to a now mechanically coherent
set of heavenly spheres, his mathematics, like al-Tusi's, laid the
groundwork for the replacement of ancient astronomy with helio-
centrism. His concepts of planetary and lunar motion are almost
identical to those of Copernicus.

To say that Copernicus employed Muslim mathematics is not to
deny the Pole's great achievement. But to give him sole credit for the
"Copernican" Revolution is a little disingenuous. The Christian clergyman had a couple of Islamic partners to help him along the way.

AL-HAYTHAM AND THE DISCOVERY OF OPTICS

No one knows the exact date when eyeglasses were invented. Most
history books claim it was sometime between 1300 and 1350, somewhere
in Italy. Usually anonymous inventors from Pisa or Venice are given the
credit. But perhaps a more logical place to look for the creator of spectacles is Fatimid Egypt, Pisa and Venice's trading partner. It was there that
the science of optics was born.

Abu Ali Al-Hasan ibn al-Haytham was born in Basra in 965.
When the upstart Fatimids were at the height of their power, al-
Haytham moved to Cairo, where he became a courtier in the caliph's
palace. A brash young scientist, al-Haytham was hoping to make a big

impression. He bragged to the caliph that he would do what the ancient Egyptians never did—irrigate the Nile and control the flooding that had been a part of Egyptian life for millenia. Impressed by the young man's ambition and inventiveness, the caliph funded the project, eagerly expecting results.

Then al-Haytham journeyed upstream and saw the Pyramids. Awestruck he realized how much he had underestimated the engineering prowess of the ancient Egyptians. If the geniuses who constructed the Pyramids could have controlled the Nile flooding, he reasoned, they would have. Crestfallen, he abandoned the project.

But there was one problem. He had taken a substantial sum of money from the caliph and squandered it in a futile adventure. The caliph was less than pleased. Al-Haytham returned to Cairo, fearing for his life. He had every reason to be afraid. The Caliph al-Hakim was notoriously brutal, perhaps even insane (see Chapter 7).

There was one way to escape an almost certain death. Al-Haytham decided to feign insanity himself. Banished from the court, he lived in poverty, reduced to copying mathematical texts for a living. When the caliph died decades later, al-Haytham was in his fifties.

His youth was gone but his intellectual ambition remained. "Truth," he wrote, "is sought for its own sake." It could only be found "in doctrines whose matter was sensible and whose form was rational." While living in obscurity, al-Haytham had formulated a credo that sounded very much like that of modern science:

> A person studying science with a view to knowing the truth ought to turn himself into a hostile critic of everything that he studies....He should criticize it from every point of view and in all its aspects. And while thus engaged in criticism he should also be suspicious of himself.

All those lost years, al-Haytham had been reading Aristotle and Ptolemy, as well as the mathematical and scientific treatises he was paid to copy for more fortunate scholars. In a book which he wrote called *Doubts on Ptolemy*, al-Haytham called the geocentric theory of planetary motion into question, stating that Ptolemy "assumed an arrangement that cannot exist," forcing the observations of his senses to fit into his "impossible" model. Al-Haytham was doing more than assimilating Greek wisdom. He was synthesizing it with the observation of his senses to create new knowledge. More than that, he created a new branch of science, devoted to the secrets of vision.

Al-Haytham had long been fascinated with light. What was it? What was vision? Did it originate in the eye, as the Greeks claimed? By refusing to accept the ancient authorities and instead basing his knowledge on experimentation, al-Haytham concluded that the Greek theory was absurd.

His hypothesis was radically different. From what he observed, light came from objects that themselves were capable of producing illumination. These he called "primary emissions." Light moved in straight lines or rays—a concept he invented. The rays of light moved "in the form of a sphere," in other words, in all directions.

Objects which happened to be in the way of primary emissions of light, like specks of dust, gave off light themselves, which al-Haytham called "secondary emissions." The light from these objects, being derived from primary emissions would thus be weaker. This concept was essentially that of secondary wavelets, "discovered" by the Dutch scientist Christiaan Huygens six hundred years later. Al-Haytham also believed that color was the product of colored bodies emanating light. Color, therefore, was not separate from light and could not be seen without it, a fact proven by modern science.

How light was perceived was another matter. Al-Haytham discovered that the eye does not send out rays of light, but instead reflects them. He even discussed the idea of an optic nerve and its relationship to the brain.

To bolster his theories al-Haytham did countless experiments: on refraction, the nature of shadows, the rectilinear motion of light, and the first mathematical study of the camera obscura. It was al-Haytham who first explained why the heavenly bodies appear larger as they near the horizon, measuring atmospheric refraction. He discovered the principle of inertia centuries before Isaac Newton, and attempted to calculate the speed of light.

To conduct his experiments, al-Haytham built a special lathe to create a variety of curved lenses and mirrors. The West came to know the lense, an Islamic invention, from al-Haytham's book, *Kitab al-manazir*, or the *Optical Thesaurus* as it was known in the Renaissance. This work was plagiarized by such luminaries as Da Vinci and Kepler and was the authority on the subject for five hundred years. Without lenses, and al-Haytham's experiments, there would have been no microscopes, magnifying glasses or telescopes. The great Muslim optician even discusses these lenses being used to read texts more clearly.

Perhaps it is possible that Italians invented the smaller version, spectacles. It is just as likely that eyeglasses, like many other supposed European inventions, are a product of the same Islamic science that produced geniuses like al-Haytham, the inventor of optics.

PRESERVING AND INVENTING

Many claim that there is nothing new in Islamic science. They borrowed this from the Greeks, that from the Hindus. It was only when Europeans got a hold of this stuff that things really started to happen.

But to say, as so many historians do, that Muslims merely "preserved" or "commented upon" scientific and mathematical knowledge is to commit that cardinal sin of history: omitting the truth. Many have denied that Islamic civilization had any inherent genius, any original, groundbreaking thought. Yet all one needs to do is look at the work of al-Battani or al-Haytham or many others to see through that ethnocentric self-deception.

Muslims are often seen as accidental custodians of Greek wisdom who bestowed this priceless treasure to its rightful heirs—the

Europeans—when the time was ripe. Nothing could be further from the truth. Muslims, far more than Christians, were responsible for not only preserving Greek science but enhancing it—daring to actually criticize Aristotle and move beyond. Their creation was modern science, Islam's greatest gift to the West.

5

Beyond
The Arabian Nights

In the nineteenth century, Europeans developed a taste for all things "oriental." Van Gogh found his inspiration in Japanese art while Rudyard Kipling made a cottage industry out of tales from India. For a wide range of artists and writers there was nowhere more alluring than the world of Islam.

This is a fantastic, exotic locale—a place of fairy tales. In its fabulous cities of minarets and onion-shaped domes live arcane sages and their genies. Aladdin rides his flying carpet, careening over sand dunes bathed in mystic moonlight. There are harems with thinly-veiled, voluptuous women lounging suggestively. Elsewhere savage, turbaned warriors sharpen their scimitars or brandish rifles while atop strident camels.

It is a sensuous land, one of strong and violent passions, where men and women live and die to age-old rhythms. Savage, sexual, threatening and enticing: this is the world of the *Arabian Nights* and the *Rubaiyyat*.

It is also primarily the world of Victorian wish-fulfillment. Rather than an accurate picture of a place or time, the Arabian Night fantasy is a projection through which the imperialist Europeans dreamed their fervid fantasies of sex and violence unrestrained by social convention. For them, the lands of Islam were utterly alien, as antithetical to Victorian London or Paris as one could imagine.

Sadly, these trappings of European fantasy continue to insinuate themselves in our culture. In the popular imagination, the Islamic world is still perceived as fundamentally different from Europe and America, its art existing like a genie in a bottle, sealed off and self-contained.

This warped vision of an inviolable, ages-stagnant culture belies a more complex reality. For Islamic art in all its variety is not alien at all, but a part of the West's cultural heritage.

ROCK N' ROLL MADE POSSIBLE

Rock music is one of the West's greatest cultural exports. The sight of Jimi Hendrix lighting his electric guitar on fire and smashing it on stage sums up all the glorious excesses of a music that has become, for better or worse, the lingua franca of adolescence. The guitar is an American icon.

It is also an Arab invention. The word itself is Arabic—*kaitara*, coming to Europe by way of al-Andalus, the Islamic kingdom of Spain. Its capital, Cordoba, was not just the most sumptuous city in all of medieval Europe but also its cultural hub, the Paris or New York of its time.

Before the Muslims, Europeans had only two stringed instruments, the rote and the harp. With the advent of the exiled Umayyads who founded al-Andalus, musicians introduced a cornucopia of new instruments, the most important being the lute, guitar and tambourine.

The lute, which defines the sound of European music through the Elizabethan period, was revolutionary in more ways than one. Beyond their novel sound, lutes came equipped with an Arab-Persian invention that changed the way stringed instruments were played and tuned. This was none other than frets on the neck, which allowed the player to tune to the Pythagorean scale, without having to solely rely on his or her ear. The lute gave birth to yet another revolutionary leap in European music, for it was while writing down music for the instrument that Muslims invented the alphabetic notation the West still uses today.

Like the lute, Arabic rhythm was daringly different. Europeans listened in rapture as a Muslim vocalist sang in one rhythm while a lute player accompanied in another. The canon technique, where one melodic line is imitated by a second starting after the first, was pioneered by Muslims and quickly absorbed by the appreciative Christians.

Europeans were so smitten with this new music that they snatched up Muslim musicians to entertain their courts. These lute players and singers had a distinctive costume that included gaudy clothes, painted faces and long hair. The Spanish word mascara comes from the Arabic word for buffoon, or minstrel. Where would all the fans of Goth and Glam bands be without the medieval Muslims?

Blackbird singing in the dead of night

In the 820s al-Andalus was still a backwater kingdom, ruled by a dynasty of Umayyads who had escaped the Abbasid's bloody purge. Within a century, however, Islamic Spain would become not only the cultural center of Europe but a caliphate to rival that of Baghdad. The process of gentrification began with the arrival in 822 of Abu al-Hasan Ali ibn Nafi.

Born in Abbasid Iraq in 789, Ali ibn Nafi became known as Ziryab, or Blackbird, for his dark complexion or melodious voice, depending on the account one reads. It is not known whether he was an African, Arab or Kurd, but it is known that he was a musician in the court of Harun al-Rashid and the disciple of Ishaq al-Mawsili, the most famous musician in Baghdad.

For a time Ziryab stayed in his master's shadow until he got his big break: the caliph summoned him to perform. Ishaq dutifully escorted his student into the caliph's presence, expecting a competent performance that would testify to the greatness of the teacher rather than the pupil.

What he did not know was that Ziryab had secretly mastered his own teacher's techniques and compositions. On top of that, he had made some innovations of his own. Declining to use his master's lute, Ziryab produced his own custom-made model, with strings of lion's cub gut and a fifth additional bass string of his own invention. The sounds he began to produce were even more exquisite due to his new pick—an eagle's claw or quill rather than the traditional wooden plectrum.

These bells and whistles would have mattered little if Ziryab had not been the consummate singer and performer. He began a composition of his own, one that no doubt incorporated his teacher's style and then went several steps beyond it. The caliph was rapturous, offering to support the brilliant young musician in the lavish manner he deserved.

Ishaq was furious, no doubt seeing the time in the not too distant future when Ziryab would replace him in the caliph's good graces. He told Ziryab to get out of Baghdad…or else.

Ziryab got the hint. He fled with his family to North Africa, forsaking the greatest city in the world for what would no doubt be a miserable exile.

It should be noted that while this romantic legend is often repeated, the more historically plausible explanation for Ziryab's flight from Baghdad may have had to do with his friendship with Caliph Amin, the son of Harun al-Rashid. Normally this would have been a desirable position. But in 819 Amin was overthrown by his brother al-Ma'mun. After the coup d'etat, the new caliph (the same one who established the House of Wisdom) let it be known that Ziryab and the rest of Amin's cronies were no longer welcome. Nevertheless Ziryab seemed to have a rare gift for ingratiating himself with powerful men. From the Maghrib, he sent an application to the ruler of al-Andalus. Receiving a warm reply, the musician packed his bags and departed, hoping his fortunes were about to take a turn for the better.

Once he arrived, however, he learned that the caliph was dead. Miserable, he prepared to return to the philistines of North Africa when fate intervened. A Jewish musician in the royal court, impressed with Ziryab's talent, put in a good word for him with the new caliph, Abd al-Rahman II. When the caliph met Ziryab, he was so taken by this cultured exile from Baghdad that he offered the lute player a yearly salary of thousands of gold pieces as well as a palace and some countryside villas. Moreover, on the two Eids and Nawruz he could expect a fat bonus. After what was no doubt a very short deliberation, Ziryab heartily accepted the offer and began to tune his lute.

Ziryab had literally hit a gold mine. But why had the caliph been so generous? It turned out that the last of the Umayyads had imperial pretensions. Like many monarchs in second-tier kingdoms, Abd al-Rahman was looking to attract first-tier talent to lend al-Andalus—and himself—prestige. Culture, as well as commerce, was a necessary component in his plan to eventually rival the Abbasids for the loyalty of all of Islam.

Soon Ziryab was holding audiences enthralled with his complex and beautiful melodies, playing the lute as they had never heard it played before. Some sources claim that Ziryab knew ten thousand songs by heart. While this is surely an exaggeration, it remains clear that his repertoire and musicianship were phenomenal, perhaps even supernaturally inspired. According to al-Maqqari:

> They relate that Ziryab used to say that the Jinn taught him music every night, and that, whenever he was thus awakened, he called his two slave-girls, Ghazzalan and Hindah, made them take their lutes, whilst he also took his, and that they passed the night conversing, playing music, and writing verses, after which they hastily retired to rest.

With the opening of his own music school—open to rich and poor alike—Ziryab effectively fathered the musical tradition of al-Andalus. Even today, the remnants of his style are still heard in flamenco and *maluf*, the classical music of Islamic North Africa.

But the young caliph got more than he bargained for when he hired Ziryab. Not only did he acquire the services of a brilliant lute player but also a socio-cultural dynamo, a fashionable innovator who created a new, sophisticated style for the Cordoban elite.

Ziryab knew the importance of cutting a fine figure in public. That was why he decided to reform the haute couture of the backwater Umayyads and introduce some Baghdad pizzazz. First off, seasonal fashions were introduced. No longer was one dreary mode of dress applicable throughout the year. For summer, white became the only acceptable color, in a variety of fabrics. For fall and winter fashionable courtiers insulated themselves in fur-trimmed cloaks. And for springtime, a rainbow of colorful silks was brought out to celebrate the thaw.

Hair was his next target. Ziryab declared the traditional long braids officially out. What he introduced was the quintessenial hairdo of the Middle Ages—the page-boy. Just try to imagine Prince Valiant in any other style.

Ziryab instructed the eager ladies in the fine art of plucking eyebrows and removing those embarassing hairs in all the wrong places. He introduced underarm deodorants and improved detergents for washing clothes. The Blackbird even set up the world's first school of cosmetology, right near Abd al-Rahman's palace, to disseminate his ideas throughout al-Andalus.

When he wasn't engaged in lute playing or fashion design, Ziryab was reforming Andalusian cuisine. Before his arrival, meals had consisted of a horde of platters, all thrown together on a bare wooden table. Now Ziryab decreed that tables would be covered with cloths of tooled-leather, which were more easily washed. On them would be served delicious and innovative new foods including forcemeat balls and a weed which Ziryab transformed into a gourmet vegetable—asparagus. Meals would no longer be a chaos of different dishes served simultaneously. Instead, he chose an order for the food to be served: first the soups and sauces, next the meats and last the desserts. This multi-course meal became the standard not just in Islamic Spain but in the whole Western world. Finally he banished ostentatious gold and silver goblets and began the trend of drinking from crystal. Think of Ziryab next time you are spooning that last appetizer before the entrée or sipping a cocktail in a tall, thin glass.

After a healthy, three course meal it was only natural to relax a little bit, perhaps to play a game of skill. Ziryab taught Abd al-Rahman and his courtiers an Indian diversion that was all the rage in Baghdad. It became known in Europe as chess.

By the time of his death in 857, Ziryab had revolutionized music in al-Andalus and created a culture of the bon vivant that would be one of the great Islamic exports to a luxury-starved Western Europe. Muslim culture did more than teach Europeans philosophy and science. It taught them how to live with style and elegance. If the good life of the civilized world has a patron saint, it is Ziryab, the Blackbird of Cordoba.

COURTLY LOVE

Most peoples' introduction to the Middle Ages comes from reading tales of King Arthur. These legendary stories seem to define the very essence of the medieval. We use them to explain even our own times: America under JFK is "Camelot," a sincere do-gooder is a "Galahad," and women long for their "knight in shining armor" to rescue them from a boring and lonely life.

The central story of the Arthur legends is the love triangle between King Arthur, Queen Guinevere and Sir Launcelot. In its tragic climax, Arthur's wife and his most trusted friend engage in a passionate affair that winds up destroying them both. During the Middle Ages, as now, this tale was a paragon of "courtly love," a bold new conception of relations between the sexes that took Europe by storm in the twelfth century.

Courtly love reinvented for Europe the Greek term *eros*, the overwhelming passion of sex—just the sort of thing that made the monks and priests shiver in their vestments. It was often adulterous and always forbidden. Being extramarital, the new ideal came into conflict with the established doctrines of the church, where holy matrimony was a sacrament. For most noble men and women, however, marriage was a stifling affair, dependent on the dynastic ambitions of parents rather than the mutual affection of their children. Many were trapped in loveless relationships that the church prevented them from dissolving. Tales of courtly love, where noble young knights worshipped their queens from afar (and sometimes not so far), became an escape valve from the depressing realities of medieval womanhood. They also served as a blueprint for a new kind of love based on the heart rather than the church or the purse-strings.

Many scholars view the emergence of courtly love in Europe as a sexual and social revolution. Friedrich Nietzsche said it proved that "love as passion is our European specialty...invented by the poet-knights of Provence...to whom Europe owes so much, and indeed, almost itself." Other writers view courtly love as the beginning of European manners and respect for womankind. Joseph Campbell, the mythology guru, claims that it was courtly love that liberated Europe from the stifling oppression of medieval Christendom and began the process of critiquing the church, leading not only to the Reformation but to the Scientific Revolution as well!

From where, then, did courtly love arise? The usual answer is Provence. It was there in southern France that William of Aquitaine (grandfather of Richard the Lionheart) began to craft the verses that, for many, created European poetry.

William wrote in the emerging vernacular. Before this time, verse was composed in Latin, the language of the church, and its structure dictated by a rigid classical tradition. To write poetry in the *langue d'oc*, the French common tongue, was thus breaking with the church's monopoly on literature. It is no surprise that the initial verses composed in French were not about *agape*, the spiritual love of Christ, but *eros*, the enflamed passion of lovers. Forbidden love became the new sacrament in a secular religion that worshipped unattainable women.

The poets who began this tradition became known as troubadours. Some were noblemen like William, who legitimized and popularized the vernacular new wave. Others were simply wandering minstrels, floating from court to court between the Alps and the Pyrenees. They sang of ladies, fair and pure of heart, who should be loved from afar. The nobility of the ladies was supposed to have an effect on their admirers, often brutal men with little social grace. It was out of such sentiments that chivalry was born.

Troubadour poetry, as revolutionary as it was, began to develop its own set of clichés. The women were always blonde and fair of skin. The men were insensate to cold or heat, hunger or pain, living only for love. The ladies were always married and always of aristocratic birth. Yet clichés have never hindered a genre's popularity. Courtly love spread throughout France and the rest of Europe. It thrilled its audiences with tales of illicit passion and sex.

The church countered with the invention of the cult of Mary. Why not worship the Mother of God from afar, the ultimate unattainable woman? At the same time, Rome waged a merciless crusade in France that wiped out the Albigensians, heretics who not only preached free love but practiced it. Try as they would, however, the Pope and his minions could not stem the tide. Love had caught on again in Europe and the tales of courtly amour became so commonplace that Miguel Cervantes would be lampooning them a few centuries later in *Don Quixote*.

But there is one question that still remains unanswered. Just where did the idea of courtly love come from? Why did it develop when it did? Most importantly, does its emergence in Provence prove for all time that the French are better lovers than the rest of us?

My old college text (Tierney and Painter's *Western Europe in the Middle Ages*) puts it the most typically: "The origins of this poetry are obscure."

Obscure, that is, if you choose to avoid the poetry of al-Andalus.

Love, Islamic Style

For most of Islamic history, poetry had been constrained by the conventions of the classical Arabic style. In its early days this poetry was fresh and original. By the time of the Western caliphate in Cordoba, however, classical poetry had become stale and derivative—a language of formalistic clichés. Smiles were always pearls, flowers were jewels, the lightning in the rain was like burning love in teardrops and so on, ad nauseam.

Love seemed to be merely going through the motions until the dynamic culture of al-Andalus got a hold of it. It was there that a blind poet named Muqaddam of Cabra decided to break the rules. Tearing apart the complicated structure of Arabic poetry piece by piece, Muqaddam and others evolved a new form of song with shortened lines, new varieties of rhyme and most shocking, a final couplet in the language of the common people—either Hebrew or more often Mozarabic, the Arabic-inflected language of the local Christians.

This was called the *muwashaha* or ring song, from the Arabic word for "sash" or "girdle." Through their new complicated structure, these songs linked Romance and Arabic in a dizzying ring of rhyme that stretched from one stanza to the next, culminating in the final ribald couplet of vernacular poetry.

But what were these songs actually about? Think of the pop songs today and you will have your answer. Love, Islamic style. Forbidden love, lost love, passionate love. And in between a healthy dose of very un-Islamic alcohol consumption. Here is an example written by Muhammad ibn Hasan al-Nawaji (d. 1455):

> Come, hand the precious cup to me
> And brim it high with a golden sea!
> Let the old wine circle from guest to guest,
> While the bubbles gleam like pearls on its breast,
> So that night is of darkness dispossessed.
> How it foams and twinkles in fiery glee!
> 'Tis drawn from the Pleiads' cluster, perdie.

Pass it, to music's melting sound,
Here on this flowery carpet round,
Where gentle dews refresh the ground
And bathe my limbs deliciously
In their cool and balmy fragrancy.

Alone with me in the garden green
A singing-girl enchants the scene:
Her smile diffuses a radiant sheen.
I cast off shame, for no spy can see,
And "Hola," I cry, "let us merry be!"

While Muslim Spain was far from a liberated society, it did give women more options than anywhere else in Europe. The domestic sphere was, as usual, their typical habitat. But education for women was not unknown, with females even lecturing on law and theology. Al-Andalus boasted many co-ed schools, where wives could attend with their husbands or daughters with their fathers. They received diplomas as the men did, entitling them to teach or open schools of their own. One prince was so taken by the intellectual accomplishments of an African slave-girl that he married her.

Many women worked as copyists, creating hand-written Qur'ans for the bookbuying public. At one point, Cordoba boasted two hundred female copyists, many of whom certainly supported their families with the income. The very idea of common women being able to read would have stunned the Christians to the North—as would the saucy poetry of noblewomen like Wallada, who composed odes to her lesbian lovers while holding a salon that nurtured an entire generation of Andalusian songsters. With the relative freedoms of Muslim Spain, it is not surprising to find the topic of love enjoying an openness that would have been unthinkable in the prudish world of Christendom.

But erotic passion was not the only theme of Andalusian poetry. A generation or two before French troubadours began plucking their lyres, the influence of Sufism began to impact Muslim Spain. This mystical branch of Islam, deriving from Persia, focused on a direct union with God through religious ecstasy. Through Sufism, the soul strove for a fusion of his being in the vast presence of the ultimate love object, God Himself.

Sufism held great appeal for the poet Muhammad ibn Da'ud al-Isfahani, born in the Eastern caliphate in the second half of the ninth century. In his youth he had fallen madly in love with a boy in his school. Tormented by his passion, which the Qur'an condemned, Ibn Da'ud found solace in the newly discovered concept of Platonic love. Ibn Da'ud's *Book of the Flower* became the blueprint for courtly love poetry in Europe.

In the last years of the Cordoban caliphate, Ibn Da'ud's philosophy thoroughly penentrated Andalusian love verse. It found its greatest expression in the *Neck-Ring of the Dove*, by Ibn Hazm. By the time of his birth in the eleventh century, the caliphate of Cordoba was losing steam. Through a series of internecine wars, Islamic Spain would be carved up into city-states known as taifas. It was in the culture of the taifas that Ibn Hazm would write his great work.

Raised in a harem, Ibn Hazm acquired a sensitivity that would see him through many idealistic struggles to restore the caliphate. Frequently imprisoned, exiled and financially ruined, Ibn Hazm finally retired from public life and devoted himself to writing. For most Muslims, he is best known as a theologian, possibly the founder of comparative religion. But for the West, it is his guide-book to the human heart that has gained the widest audience.

In the *Neck-Ring* we see the courtly world of vanished Cordoba spring back to life. There, graceful maidens (usually blonde—Ibn Hazm's preference) and their gallant lovers struggle through the labyrinth of passion. In prose and poetry, Ibn Hazm lays out the life cycle of love, from the first encounters in dreams and sight, to conveying emotions through the eyes and other secret signals, and on to the helpers that bear messages and those who seek to prevent the inevitable. Ibn Hazm describes the ultimate union of the two as better than anything on Earth, better than "the favor of the sultan and the privilege of wealth, or being something after being nothing, or return after long exile, or safety after fear." Ibn Hazm knew what he was talking about. He had experienced all of these emotions as well as the worst tragedy, the death of a slave girl who was the love of his life, one whose memory he never forgot.

Thus Ibn Hazm concludes with a chapter on chastity, the love from afar that was the only love possible for him now, with his girl and kingdom gone. This union of souls was the highest, purest form of passion. Culling numerous examples of rapturous, Platonic affection from al-Andalus, Ibn Hazm falls in squarely with Ibn Da'ud. Platonic, spiritual love is to be the new ideal. Perhaps as a consolation for the many losses he suffered, Ibn Hazm proclaims that "greater shall be the reward of him that hid in his heart a hotter flame than embers of tamarind, who has suffered in his inward parts a laceration keener than the sword!" This Platonic ethos, born of Ibn Da'ud's odes to forbidden passion, became the new love song of Europe. Ibn Hazm's most famous disciple was Andreas Cappelanus, the author of *The Art of Courtly Love*, a twelfth-century work clearly modeled on the earlier, Muslim one.

Within a generation after Ibn Hazm's death, the singers and poets of the taifas crossed the Pyrenees. Many of them were prizes of war. With al-Andalus weakened by internal strife, Christians had gained ground. At the Battle of Barbastro in 1064, thousands of women were taken captive and transported to southern France. Many of these women were *qiyan*, professional singers who made a living from the muwashaha. Barbastro, and other battles like it, opened a cultural door between France and Spain that allowed the light of Islam's culture to illumine Christendom. It is hardly a coincidence that William of Aquitaine, the father of Provencal poetry, was the son of the man who won Barbastro. It was in his father's court that he would hear the songs of a lost world that would, in turn, give birth to a new literature and a new kind of love.

Dante's Night Journey

The Divine Comedy of Dante Alighieri (1265-1321) is one of the masterpieces of Western literature. In its three books, *Hell, Purgatory* and *Paradise*, Dante made the afterlife palpable, mapping its horrors and ecstasies in a narrative that was as realistic as it was ineffably spiritual. The *Comedy* was the supreme expression of Christian hope and faith, a spiritual pilgrimage for author and reader. An Italian national treasure and a catalogue of Catholic orthodoxy, the *Comedy* sums up everything that Western society stood for in the Middle Ages.

It almost sounds like sacrilege to say it then: the plot of the *Divine Comedy* is largely borrowed from Islamic literature, as are many of its characters, incidents, descriptions and philosophies. This masterpiece of Western literature is in essence an imitation, a Muslim poem with Christian window-dressing.

It all goes back to the Qur'an, Surah 17:1: "Glory be to Him who made His servant [Muhammad] go by night from the Sacred Temple to the farther Temple whose surroundings We have blessed, that We might show him some of Our signs."

This is the only mention in the Qur'an of Muhammad's '*Isra*, or mystical Night Journey, a visionary experience where the Prophet traveled from Arabia to Jerusalem in one night. From there, on the remains of the Jewish Temple, he ascended into heaven, an event known in Islam as the *Mir'aj*. The Dome of the Rock in modern-day Jerusalem marks the spot where he stepped from this world into the next. Over the centuries, a rich body of lore developed around this tradition. It was this literature that served as Dante's blueprint and inspiration.

In his book, *Islam and the Divine Comedy*, Miguel Asin Palacios made an exhaustive list of similarities between Dante's *Comedy* and Muslim accounts of the 'Isra and Mir'aj, especially those of a Cordoban poet, Muhyi al-Din Abu Bakr Muhammad ibn al-Arabi (1165-1240) in his book *Al-Futuhat al-Makkiyah*, The Revelations of Mecca. Written 25 years before Dante was born, Ibn al-Arabi's work provides not just themes but a plethora of details that would be used in the later Christian poem. What is especially interesting is that Ibn al-Arabi breaks from tradition and puts himself in Muhammad's place. As in Dante's later account, it is a mere sinner who begins the mystical pilgrimage rather than an important religious figure.

Both accounts commence at night, when the narrator is suddenly awakened by the spiritual guide. They proceed to the gate of hell which is guarded by a lion and a wolf (Dante adds a leopard). Once inside they find that hell is funnel-shaped, with concentric stories occupied by increasingly worse kinds of sinners, from adulterers to sodomites to heretics and traitors. Here in this nightmarish world, decapitated souls walk around with their talking heads in hand or with their bowels protruding, are perishing of thirst or prodded by demons with forks into seas of boiling pitch or flame.

For the damned, the punishment fits the crime. Carnal sinners are tossed about by a great whirlwind symbolizing their passion. Murderers boil in the blood they were so fond of shedding. The sins get progressively worse the deeper they go and so do the punishments: torturing serpents, swollen bellies, leprous scabs that constantly itch and flake off, murderous demons stabbing bodies to pieces only to reconstitute them for another go. Along the way, the narrators meet the great thinkers and notorious celebrities of their respective traditions, with whom they have learned discussions. At the bottom of hell Satan is immersed in a lake of ice.

As the visitors emerge from the inferno, they wash themselves three times in waters that separate hell from purgatory. Muslims, like Catholic Christians, conceived of an afterlife where some were damned forever, some only for a time till they were purified and some others blessed enough to be sent straight to paradise. From here the pilgrims toil up a steep mountain, encountering an awful hag who tries to halt their progress. But with the help of their guide, they make it to the gates of paradise where they meet a beautiful maiden.

It is interesting to note that for Dante, this maiden is none other than Beatrice, the great Platonic love of his life whom he immortalized in his *La Vita Nuova*. Not too surprisingly, Ibn al-Arabi also had written Platonic love poems about Nizam, a beautiful girl whom he met in Mecca. In his book *The Interpreter of Longings* he takes the theme of lost love and transforms it into a mystical allegory of divine beauty and the soul's quest for God—exactly as Dante was to do half a century later.

In the last stage of their celestial journey, both authors depict Paradise as a series of nine heavens, ranked by virtues. A glorious light grows more radiant the further they climb. Heroes and martyrs from the respective faiths, some grouped by their circle of literature, hold forth on erudite topics or simply tell their life's story. Two women, personally known to the poets, tell of their troubles in married life while the visitors stand awestruck by their beauty.

As they reach the last stage of ascension, their guides depart. Suddenly they are whisked into the highest heaven, where they encounter a celestial creature in the shape of a bird, flapping its wings and calling all creation to prayer. Afterwards they behold a ladder, on which the blessed souls are ascending and descending.

From here, the wanderers look downwards and are amazed by how small the world is compared to the heavenly cosmos. Around them angels made of fire and snow swirl about the throne of God. At first blinded by His magnificence the visitors slowly make out the angels revolving around Him like the celestial spheres in space. From afar they behold the awesome spectacle and then, drawing closer, they are finally immersed in the all-encompassing light of the Divine Presence.

These poems are not tales of horror and wonder for mere amusement. They are guidebooks for the regeneration of the soul, illustrated in graphic detail. For the Sufi mystic Ibn al-Arabi as well as Dante, eternal truth cannot be attained by human reason but by the light of God's grace.

This was a point Dante felt he needed to make. This zealous defender of the church saw the medieval age of faith cracking apart at its foundations. The cause of the distress was clear. Islam, in so many ways, was dismantling all that the church stood for. The Crusades had recently been aborted with the Muslims victorious. Europeans in the meantime had acquired an unquenchable passion for luxury goods from Egypt and Arabia: plates, carpets, clothes, books, ceramics. Perhaps worst of all monks, professors and others were learning Arabic and proclaiming Muslim philosophy to be superior to Christian thinking. With its values firmly grounded in natural science and human reason, "Arabist" philosophy was the single greatest threat to Dante's most sacred beliefs.

It is possible that Dante acquired his knowledge of Islam and specifically Ibn al-Arabi through his mentor and teacher Brunetto Latini. In 1260, Latini became Florence's ambassador to Spain. At the capital in Toledo, he would have certainly come in contact with the vast libraries of Arabic manuscripts and their translations. When he returned to Florence Latini composed several works which quoted Muslim writers and incorporated their ideas. It is interesting to note that Dante puts the soul of this open-minded scholar, mentor and dear friend in Hell.

Yet try as he would Dante could not escape the impact of Islamic thought. In his works he frequently quotes Ibn Sina and Ibn Rushd, even placing them in Limbo where they can join forces with the greats of ancient Greece and Rome. But his admiration only goes so far.

In *Inferno*, Dante has reached just about the lowest part of hell. There he meets a disembowelled man, torn in two. The pathetic, mutilated figure spots Dante and exposes his wounds in a gory spectacle. Before him walks another, similarly disfigured, his face split from "chin to forelock."

Muslims would no doubt recoil in disgust at this repulsive description of their Prophet and Ali, literally split apart in revenge for dividing the Christian world. It expresses the loathing and hatred that many Europeans, including Dante, must have felt for the people who seemed to be vanquishing them on all fronts: political, economic, cultural and philosophical. Which is precisely why, according to scholars like Maria Rosa Menocal, Dante may have been moved to write the *Divine Comedy*. Perhaps his great epic poem is a desperate last jab at Islam, a negative image of its religious traditions that could deflect the influence of Arabism and restore the church's monopoly on thought. If that was his aim, Dante ultimately failed, as did all of medieval Christendom. The cultural and scientific accomplishments of the Muslims would reshape Europe into its modern form.

Yet over the centuries, their influence would be forgotten. It was a process begun here quite consciously in Dante's reworking of the 'Isra and Mir'aj. By putting a Christian face on the earlier Muslim accounts, he slowly began to erase the traces of his hated rivals. In time, with the help of later Renaissance writers, Europeans could feel confident in their own genius, never having to admit it sprang not from a vacuum or the rediscovery of ancient Greece, but from the heart of the enemy they still loathed and feared.

Is Dante's work still a masterpiece? Of course. He incorporates many original elements into Ibn al-Arabi's framework, building as all great artists do on a preexisting tradition, creating a vivid and vernacular picture of thirteenth and fourteenth century Italian society. Nevertheless, the evidence is clear. Muslim theology and literature directly influenced—on every level of plot, character and theme—the greatest poem in European history. That most still remain ignorant of the vast debt owed to Ibn al-Arabi and others is a testament to the enduring prejudice of Western scholarship.

6

Islam's Secret Weapon

Questioning authority was not considered very polite in the Middle Ages, especially when it was the authority of the church. Over intellectual matters, the Holy See held a monopoly. Anything that would not conform to Catholic doctrine was banned. Anyone who defied that ban was in danger of imprisonment, excommunication or death. The *auto da fé* or public burning of heretics became a common sight in medieval Europe. "Heretic" meant anyone foolish enough to question the Catholic Church.

The church decided which books and authors could be read. It decided which doctrines were true and which were false. And it even decided in which language the Bible could be read and reproduced. Anyone who dared to translate the Bible could be executed in a public act of terror designed to intimidate an already superstitious and ignorant population.

No doubt the clerics thought they were doing the right thing. The church had to survive at all costs. In this world of sin and temptation, the Devil exercised a fearsome power that must be met with an equally vicious fortitude. Naturally the struggle for the church meant the struggle to preserve its vast land holdings, serfs and staggering wealth. The Pope could make kings grovel by even threatening excommunication. He maintained armies, collected hordes of money from rich and poor alike and owned the vast majority of the Italian peninsula. The church was by far the largest landholder in all of Europe.

With all this at stake, Rome was not about to allow any challenges to its spiritual authority which was, after all, the reason for its revenues. If certain ideas began to take hold in the popular mind, it would not be too long before people not only lost faith, but the church lost its land and its income. Their fears, of course, were justified.

The effects were not instantaneous, not even after Luther wrote his ninety-five theses. But by the modern era, the Catholic Church had lost its spiritual monopoly and was forced to begin an aggressive missionary program to acquire new members in strange and exotic lands. In Europe, despite its best efforts, the church lost ground to the Scientific Revolution, which not only propelled Europeans into modernity but also posed the greatest philosophical threat to the very existence of faith itself.

History is full of ironies. One of the greatest of them is that the Islamic world, which the church had helped to destabilize and impoverish intellectually and financially, would deal that same church a near death blow by introducing a secret weapon: Aristotle.

The Greek Heritage of Islam

It is a truism of Western scholarship that Muslims "preserved" Greek texts to hand over to their rightful heirs, the Christian Europeans, centuries later. This begs the question: what did the Muslims do with all that philosophy for five centuries?

First, let's use a different term than "preserve." Let's use "nurture" or "save" or maybe even better, "reinvent." Muslims were not simply passive recipients of alien wisdom. They were the ones who inherited the Greek intellectual center of Alexandria in 641 and drew upon its scholars to provide them with not only Plato's writings but also all that we have left of Aristotle's. It was to Persia where the scholars of

Plato's Academy fled when the Christian emperor Justinian closed it in a fit of pious indignation. And at the same time, Syriac-speaking Nestorian Christians living in the Middle East had long cultivated a Neoplatonist tradition, drawing on the works of Plotinus and others who synthesized Greek philosophy with Eastern mysticism.

Muslims didn't simply blunder into a secret library containing the Greek classics and stare at them for five centuries, scratching their heads. Almost immediately after conquering Greek and Persian territory, Muslim scholars began to methodically search for philosophical manuscripts and labored to integrate them with their own religious traditions. In short, *they made Greek philosophy their own.* This was the great work of Islamic scholarship and thought in the few centuries before the first millenium.

THE UNBEARABLE LIGHTNESS OF FORMS

The two heavy-hitters of Greek philosophy were Plato (427-347 BC) and his most brilliant pupil, Aristotle (384-322 BC). Plato believed that the only things in the universe that were truly real were the forms, or ideas. These forms, like the Good, the True and the Beautiful, are the essence of every material thing. What passes for good, true and beautiful in our physical world is a mere reflection, a shadow, of the perfect, transcendent forms. Plato illustrates this principle in his famous "allegory of the cave." In this story, people inhabit a cave wherein they are chained to a rock. A fire burns behind them which they cannot turn their heads to see. Whenever something passes before the fire they take for real the shadow that is cast on the wall before them. Only when souls have been freed from their chains will they see the true reality—the Ideas that cast their reflection in the physical objects of our world. For Plato, life is a journey of remembrance, a quest to reestablish contact with the eternal Forms and thus the eternal within us.

If Plato had Ideas then Aristotle had Categories. People, for example, while very different as individuals, could all be classed under the category of "person." But in Aristotle's world, a human was not a mere shadow of the transcendent "Person." Form did not transcend matter at all. It was bound within it, providing matter with a goal for development. Matter moved from potentiality to actuality, its ultimate purpose to realize the form within itself.

Forms then were not somewhere out there, beyond our senses. They could be observed in the physical world, in the universal patterns which governed particular objects. If the natural world is not observed, no actual knowledge can be discovered, since the underlying forms are intrinsically joined with material reality.

Yet Aristotle was not a strict materialist. Just as substances held within them a form that motivated them to perfection, so too did the universe have a form within itself and from which it derived its existence. Aristotle called this the divine intellect, from which stemmed our human intellect. The divine intellect enabled humans to see the patterns and ultimate goals of the universe. While the individual soul, since it was bound up with the body, would perish at death, the part of us that belonged to the divine intellect would return to its eternal source.

The two philosophies could not be more different: Plato distrusts the senses, Aristotle depends on them. Plato sees the truly real as somehow beyond our physical world, whereas Aristotle sees the real within our world. And while the Platonic soul is immortal, Aristotle's is perishable, with only the impersonal and eternal spark of the divine intellect surviving death.

Not surprisingly, Plato's more mystical approach was far more popular with Christians, especially in the West. During the Middle Ages, Plato was well known in Europe. Aristotle, on the other hand, had a relatively small reputation. Virtually none of his works existed in Latin form. In the Islamic world, however, scholars had access to what remained of his entire oeuvre. For Muslims, Aristotle simply became known as The Philosopher, the greatest of them all. And his philosophy was so troubling that it sparked controversy from the moment it was translated into Arabic.

For Muslims as well as Christians, there were certain basic truths that everyone believed through faith. They knew there was a God, that he had created the world from nothing at a specific point in time and that when people died they would be resurrected, bodily, to paradise or torment. None of these things could be proved scientifically, but this did not trouble most Muslims. There was human wisdom—which was discernible to mortals—and then there was the divine wisdom of Allah. The Qur'an was a revelation from God Himself which had no need of being proved or disproved. Yet according to Aristotle, the rules of logic which governed the entire cosmos could be grasped by mortal beings. These rules seemed to come in direct conflict with Islamic revelation.

While this is just the tip of the iceberg, the implications are already calamitous. God's creation of the world from nothing was suddenly rendered illogical. For Aristotle the universe was without beginning or end. How was it logical, after all, for nothing (the absence of being by definition) to generate being? If the universe operated by certain discernible laws or patterns, then miracles were a logical contradiction as well. If a person's soul is tied to their physical body then it appears as if the soul is not immortal. Worst of all, if truth can be known through an inherent active intellect and sensory perception of the natural world, who needs the Qur'an?

Clearly something had to be done about this. Scholars could have simply banned Aristotle, as the Catholic Church did in the early 1200s. But Muslims could see the incredible benefits of Aristotle's system—what it allowed them to think, to do and to discover. Logic worked and so did human reason when basing its conclusions on observation of the natural world. Scientists were soon using Aristotle's philosophy to reinvent science itself. They thought little of what Aristotle ultimately meant for their faith. They simply knew that he got them results.

It fell to a series of theologians and philosophers to grapple with the spiritual ramifications of these earth-shattering theories.

THE FIRST ARAB PHILOSOPHER

Abu-Yusuf Ya'qub ibn Ishaq al-Kindi (795-866) was the first genuine Islamic philosopher, an Arab thinker who created a new worldview (as St. Thomas Aquinas would centuries later) that harmonized his religious tradition with the Greeks. In his truly prodigious output—a total of three hundred and sixty-one works—al-Kindi demonstrated that faith and reason were not incompatible. In fact, he claimed, the truth revealed by Muhammad was backed up by logic, which theologians should not shun but use as a spiritual tool. Prophets and philosophers might come by knowledge in different ways, but the truths they demonstrated were the same. It was just that philosophers had to prove their truths, while prophets didn't.

Aristotle is true, al-Kindi might say, because we can see the results in the world. And so is the Qur'an, because we can see the results in our hearts. But how did he reconcile the vast differences between the two?

A student of his once asked him if the Qur'an made any sense when it said in Surah 55:6: "The stars and the trees offer worship." It just didn't seem to be the kind of thing stars and trees were capable of doing. But al-Kindi responded by looking at the definition of "to offer worship." In this case, he said that this verb, *yasjud*, simply meant to grow and develop as God has ordained. To offer worship then, al-Kindi claimed, meant simply for the stars and trees to obey God's commands for their behavior, which perfectly harmonizes with Aristotle's concept of the universe obeying fixed natural laws.

Al-Kindi did something few had dared to do before. He used philosophy to liberate the Qur'an from close-minded literalism. It was a giant leap toward a more enlightened spirituality and a more complex world. And it was a way for religion to still make some kind of sense to those for whom logic and reason had taken the place of blind faith.

PHYSICIAN AND PHILOSOPHER

While some radical philosophers like al-Razi disavowed revelation completely, others began to gravitate toward a more mystical kind of philosophy. Its foremost proponent was none other than Ibn Sina, the star physician and intellect who towers so high in Islamic history that Iran and other nations claim him as one of their own—although he was born in what is today Uzbekistan.

Ibn Sina became interested in philosophy as a youth while listening to his brother and father discuss the newest fad: Neopythagoreanism. Pythagoras is familiar to most school students as the originator of the theorem $a^2 + b^2 = c^2$. But he did far more than think about triangles. In fact, he was the leader of a cult that worshipped numbers as divine principles that mirrored the nature of reality. All this mystical talk whetted Ibn Sina's appetite for a Pythagoras-inspired philosophy from the third century AD that had been popular for centuries.

This was known as Neoplatonism. It was largely the work of Plotinus, a follower of Plato who sought to combine the philosophy of Greece with the mystical traditions of the East. Like Plato, Plotinus sought union with transcendent ideas, all of which were contained in "the One." Creation began through a process known as "emanation." From the One emanated the Intellect, then the Soul. This emanation was, according to Plotinus, like light from a candle, gradually getting darker. We are on the dark end, far from the source and yet still a part of it. By recognizing this eternal process of emanation and return, the human mind can attain liberation from the physical world and head back to the One, where subject and object are the same.

Ibn Sina took this New Age-style philosophy and attempted to harmonize it with Islam. First he put God in the place of the One. Now Allah was doing the emanating in an eternal cycle. Next he set about to logically prove the existence of God, as had Aristotle before him.

Aristotle's proof of God went as follows. The universe was characterized by change, from potential being to actual being. Motion was behind all kinds of change. Whatever moved had to have something causing its motion. Taken to the cosmic level, the universe itself needed to have something causing it to change and develop from potentiality to actuality. This was the Unmoved Mover.

The Unmoved Mover, unlike the rest of the universe, was pure actuality. It was eternal and immutable and separate from the material world of change. It sounds much like Plato's concept of Forms with this crucial difference: Aristotle did not see the physical world as a mere shadow of the Unmoved Mover, a fraudulent knock-off. Rather it was a reflection, a testament to the divine cause of which it was the effect. By studying nature, we could see the traces of this universal source.

Ibn Sina could see some problems in Aristotle's cosmology, especially from the Islamic viewpoint. If God was somehow separate from material creation then miracles were out of the question. God couldn't suspend physical laws because it was impossible for him to be here, in the physical universe. Not to mention the fact that if the universe were eternal and God were eternal then how could he have done any creating?

Perhaps everything could be resolved by saying God was not so much an Unmoved Mover as a Necessary Existent. Rather than focus on motion and change, Ibn Sina used the concepts of essence and existence, cause and effect, to make his proof. Essence is what defines a thing while existence is its being, or the potential for it. What is the cause and what is the effect? It's akin to the question, "Which comes first, the chicken or the egg?"

Sooner or later, by infinitely regressing, you would reach a being whose definition was the same as its being. And that would be, you guessed it, God. He exists because both categories have to start from somewhere. For Ibn Sina then, God is necessary, the cause of all. Everything else in the universe is contingent—an effect depending on something else—part of that cycle of essence to existence and back again.

Next he had to tackle the soul. Like Aristotle, Ibn Sina believed the soul contained a part of the divine intellect. But in Ibn Sina's case, the divine intellect happened to be God. This led him to a parting of ways with Aristotle, for whom the soul was material. For if the soul contained a part of God in its essence, it must be immortal. How could part of God *not* be immortal?

Still, bodily resurrection was out. He agreed with Aristotle and Plotinus that the universe was eternal. If that was the case then there could be no "end of time" for the resurrection to occur as it says in the Qur'an. Did that imply that the holy book was in error?

Not at all, Ibn Sina countered. Prophets like Jesus and Muhammad had to tailor their revelations to suit the needs of their listeners. There were literal meanings intended for the slow-minded and spiritual, and allegorical language for the mentally gifted. If Muhammad mentions the resurrection of the body, it is only because the masses can't grasp the spiritual intricacies of what he's really trying to say. The intellectual elite however have no such problems. Ibn Sina, while affirming bodily resurrection in a work for the popular audience, flatly rejected it in a more esoteric work.

While Ibn Sina, like al-Kindi, attempted to reconcile the two divergent worldviews of revelation and reason, it is clear that he sided more with Aristotle than Muhammad. Far less prone to compromise than al-Kindi, Ibn Sina followed philosophy's natural train of thought to create a universe that seemed at odds with some of the most sacred tenets of Islam: God's omniscience, the finite nature of the world, and the resurrection of the body. It was a challenge that could not go unanswered.

Revelation over Reason

It fell to Abu-Hamid Muhammad al-Ghazali to answer that challenge. Few figures in Islamic history have been more adored or despised. To some he is the greatest of Muslim thinkers, a theologian whose influence is still felt today, nearly a thousand years after his death. To others he is the "executioner" of philosophy, a religious fanatic whose writings helped to destroy rationalism in Islam and usher in a dark age of fundamentalism.

Al-Ghazali was born in Persia in 1058 and by the age of thirty-three was teaching theology at Baghdad's university. He was an incredibly popular instructor and a brilliant scholar, lecturing to three hundred at a time. After holding the position for only four years, he went through a crisis of the heart and soul, a spiritual nervous breakdown. Repudiating all that he had stood for, he left the bookish world of the university and became a mystic.

For some time al-Ghazali had been questioning everything: theology, law, philosophy, dogma, tradition. What he wanted was the *truth*—and more than that, the very nature of things. But rather than follow the Greek path, searching for definitions and laws that pointed to ultimate truth, al-Ghazali decided instead to "try to find what knowledge really is." The question was not, as the Greeks had said, "What is true?" but, "How do I *know* what is true?"

Al-Ghazali was not happy with simple probability. He wanted absolute certainty, and the more he thought about what he knew, the more he realized none of it was very certain. He asked himself if sense-perception gave truth. No, he decided, for senses can be tricked, as when the eyes perceive the shadow cast by a sundial as immobile while in fact it moves. Perhaps intellectual truths, then? No, again. For didn't dreams seem as real as the physical world while he was dreaming them? Was he capable of telling the difference between one or the other? "Perhaps," he said, "life in this world is a dream..."

What is truly remarkable here is that most students of Western philosophy have heard these arguments before. They are identical to the *Meditations* of Rene Descartes, considered by many to be the first modern philosopher. The textbooks extol Descartes' epoch-making decision to move from cosmology, the study of the universe, to epistemology, the study of knowledge. They marvel at his ponderings on how he knows what he knows, what is certain, and whether or not knowledge is even possible. For many, this is the man who ushered in the Enlightenment, the whole modern worldview. And here is al-Ghazali, the so-called "executioner" of philosophy, saying the same exact things—only five hundred fifty years earlier.

So why do rationalists excoriate al-Ghazali? Because in the end, he did not decide that the only certainty was: I think, therefore I am.

For al-Ghazali, *God* was the certainty he had been looking for. Whatever was true came from God. Al-Ghazali encountered this in a spiritual flash of insight, where he experienced the absolute truth as "a light which God most high cast into my breast." Truth could not be sought. Rather, it was bestowed by God in a mystic revelation that was beyond logic, proof, or sensory perception.

Interestingly, Rene Descartes—the consummate modern thinker—also claimed that God was the ultimate source of truth. The only difference between him and the Persian mystic was that for Descartes, God's existence validated human reason as a truth-detector. He reasoned that God, being perfect and good, would not give people reason only to then deceive them by it. To some, it would no doubt be disturbing to notice just how much these vastly different thinkers have in common.

But al-Ghazali, unlike Descartes, saw philosophy as largely a waste of time. As a system for discovering truth, it appeared painfully inadequate. It did not address the spiritual hunger within him. This is precisely the reason why logic and faith have never formed a more perfect union. One appeals to the mind, the other to the heart. Perhaps both systems had things to offer. Certainly al-Ghazali knew all the logical tricks of the philosopher's trade, and used them to great effect in his writing. For too long the philosophers had held complete sway over intellectual discourse. It was time to cut them down to size.

Their come-uppance came in the form of al-Ghazali's devastating critique, *The Incoherence of the Philosophers*. In it, he finally met Aristotle and Ibn Sina head on. Point after point, twenty in all, he refuted their arguments for an eternal world and a non-physical resurrection. In one of his most prescient attacks, he anticipated yet another Enlightenment philosopher, David Hume, by proving that effects do not necessarily follow from causes.

One of the main points of the philosophers was that God, being universal, could have no knowledge of the particulars of how the universe functioned. The world was deterministic and free will was illusory since natural law (the inherent categories of Aristotle) dictated the way things would exist and develop. This not only contradicted the Qur'an but also common sense. People appeared to be able to make choices affecting their own destiny. Still, the philosophers attempted to prove a link between the universal and the particular through logic. Al-Ghazali demonstrated the futility of this quest.

Ibn Sina's concept of God as a *necessary* God made no sense. Hadn't Aristotle said that the world was one of potentiality? Then how, al-Ghazali asked, could necessity, the "must be," exist in a world that by definition was only one of potentiality, the "could be?" Using their own logic, al-Ghazali dealt them a crushing blow, demonstrating that God could not be proven rationally—a primary goal of philosophers for a millenium. By the end of his book, the results are fairly conclusive: al-Ghazali: 20, Philosophers: 0.

It took a hundred years or so for the rematch. The setting was the other side of the world, in al-Andalus.

THE INCOHERENCE OF THE INCOHERENCE

One of the most famous philosophers of Muslim Spain was Abu Bakr ibn 'Abd al-Malik ibn Tufayl (c. 1116-84). He is best known for his philosophical fantasy, *Hayy ibn Yaqzan* (The Living One, Son of the Vigilant). Abandoned at birth, Hayy is raised on a desert island by a doe. Utterly alone except for his animal companions, Hayy teaches himself to survive and even learns the laws of nature by employing the scientific method of observation and experimentation. He soon learns that what sets him apart from the other creatures is his power of reason. Hayy uses his rational mind to achieve numerous insights, even teaching a newcomer to the island, Absal.

Like many other Muslim philosophers, Ibn Tufayl anticipated Descartes' emphasis on rationalism by hundreds of years. But his influence was even more far-reaching, for his work inspired another tale of a lonely castaway and his companion on a desert isle. The book was none other than Daniel Defoe's *Robinson Crusoe*, published just eleven years after Ibn Tufayl's original was translated into English in 1708.

His greatest influence on the world, however, was not his literary works but a certain friendship. As physician and courtier to the Almohads, Ibn Tufayl was able to secure a position in court for this friend, whose image would later adorn an unlikely place, far to the east.

Ibn Tufayl's friend is now the Vatican's only Muslim resident. Visitors have been noticing him there since around 1510, as a part of the august assembly known as "The School of Athens." Painted by the Renaissance genius, Raphael, the fresco shows the great thinkers of the ages, with Plato and Aristotle forming the center focus. Toward the bottom is the man who made not only Aristotle's name famous in Europe but his own as well. Medieval Christendom knew him as Averroes, the Commentator. His true name was Abu al-Walid Muhammad Ibn Rushd and he was the greatest philosopher in Europe. Responding to the challenge of al-Ghazali, Ibn Rushd would start a revolution that would destroy medievalism and usher in the modern world as we know it

He was born in Cordoba in 1126 to a prestigious family of lawyers and judges. At the university in Cordoba, with a library containing almost half a million volumes, Ibn Rushd studied his familial profession, specializing in law and medicine. After graduating he practiced in al-Andalus as well as Marrakush in North Africa. It was there that the Berbers, African Muslims who had conquered the taifa states, held their court. While the Berbers were puritanical in their religion, they strongly supported philosophy. With the help of Ibn Tufayl, Ibn Rushd was offered a judgeship in Seville, with the understanding that he would privately tutor the Berber sultan on the relatively inscrutable writings of Aristotle. With the ruler's patronage, he soon moved back to Cordoba, where he passed a pleasant decade. In 1182 he became the sultan's personal physician until the ruler's death three years later.

It was with the succession of the sultan's son, al-Mansur, that Ibn Rushd's fall from grace began. In 1195, Ibn Rushd was banished from Cordoba and his books of philosophy were burned. It is only thanks to the Jewish community, who had translated his works into Hebrew, that we can read the commentaries that so enraged his ruler. While reinstated two years later, Ibn Rushd died soon after in 1198, only a few decades before his ideas hit the European consciousness like a brick through a plate glass window.

What was it that caused the abrupt banishment and disgrace? Only what Ibn Rushd had been doing all those years when he got off work—writing commentaries on Aristotle.

The word "commentary" does not really do him justice. Far from a series of tedious margin notes on the Greek thinker, Ibn Rushd's writings are essentially meditations, original works of philosophy that use Aristotle as a starting-off point.

Aside from the commentaries, his most famous work is the *Tahafut al-Tahafut*, the *Incoherence of the Incoherence*—a direct counterattack to al-Ghazali. In it he addressed al-Ghazali's main objections to philosophy: an eternal universe based on causality, God's ignorance of the details of creation, and the denial of bodily resurrection. Here are Ibn Rushd's counter-arguments to al-Ghazali:

(1) If the universe were created at a specific time then that would seem to limit God's power. It would imply that God was forced to create it when he did. Otherwise, why not do it sooner? Or later? And how, Ibn Rushd wonders, can al-Ghazali reject causality—the whole system of natural laws that makes the universe go 'round? For it is, after all, a system that Allah Himself put in motion. To reject His system is to reject Him, isn't it?

(2) God's knowledge of the particulars of creation is non-sensical. Being God, His knowledge is necessarily different from ours. His knowledge is of the design, ours of the particulars. God is the cause, we are the effects. Knowledge can't be the same for both God and people. Ibn Rushd astutely proves his point by citing the Qur'an, Surah 6:163 which says that God has no partner. Does this rule out free will? Not at all, he maintains. While humans do have a plethora of choices, they are nevertheless choices made within certain constraints, namely natural laws. Human behavior is predicated on both nature and nurture, a decidedly modern response to the issue.

(3) Like Ibn Sina and other Muslim philosophers, Ibn Rushd reaffirmed the harmony between reason and faith. The Qur'an, he said, was composed of certain verses that the Prophet had called "sound," meant to be taken literally. Others were obviously more ambiguous and required philosophy to interpret them. Theologians and the masses couldn't truly comprehend the real meaning. This included the sections dealing with a "bodily resurrection," which were, to Ibn Rushd, symbolic ways to explain a new state of being incomprehensible to creatures in a physical world.

It was a staggering argument and a major comeback for Islamic philosophy. If he had not squarely bested al-Ghazali, Ibn Rushd had at the very least fought him to a stalemate.

After rallying against the conservative theologians, Ibn Rushd grew a little cocky. He decided to take on a tougher opponent. His chosen battleground was no longer religion but politics. At the twilight of his life, he decided to write a commentary on Plato's *The Republic*.

One of the great masterpieces of philosophy, *The Republic* is the crowning achievement of Greek thought. It is Plato's blueprint for the ideal self and the ideal society. Ibn Rushd could have used his commentary to simply explain all of the wonderful intricacies of this classic work.

But he went further. Like his commentaries on Plato's pupil, Ibn Rushd used *The Republic* not only to discuss the perfect state but also to show how the current one, the Berber Almohad dynasty, was deviating far from that ideal.

Many writers over the years have claimed that Ibn Rushd's fall from grace was caused by religious fundamentalists who were appalled by his rationalism. After Ibn Rushd, they point out, philosophy was extinguished in the Muslim world. It was the victory of fanaticism over logic, a clear-cut reason for Islam's decline on the socio-cultural stage.

In fact, Ibn Rushd did not suffer from religious oppression. His anti-theological works had been circulating for decades. Rather it was his work of political philosophy, the commentary on *The Republic*, that got his books burned. In it, he advocated wild, revolutionary reforms: the rights of women, the dissolution of marriage as a social institution, public education and evenly-distributed wealth. Worse, he dared to attack the Berber rulers of al-Andalus, branding them as decadent tyrants who had lost the consent of the governed, the very people who had given them the right to rule in the first place. It was a plea for social justice that would enflame such latter-day thinkers as

Rousseau, Jefferson and Marx. For struggling against despotism and ignorance, he was made a renegade, his reputation and spirit destroyed. Contrary to the commonly-held view in the West, it was politics far more than faith that dealt him the death blow.

Thankfully his light did not extinguish, even when his books were nothing but char and ash. Sparks had drifted northward and eastward, borne by Jewish disciples and from them to Christians, eager for a new way of looking at the world.

AVERROISM

It didn't take long for Christendom to see the storm clouds gathering. The church made a few pre-emptive strikes. In 1210 Aristotle was banned in Paris. In 1231 Pope Gregory IX convened a special commission to decide which parts of Aristotle were worth preserving and which weren't. While the commission made its study, Aristotle was banned through all of Christendom. In 1263 the ban was renewed by the next Pope. But try as the church might, the study of Aristotle went on clandestinely. So did the study of his commentator Ibn Rushd, the one who translated him, explained him, and made him live.

This Muslim tradition was absolutely essential in helping Greek learning gain popularity in Christian Europe. Ibn Rushd's thought described a centuries-long dialogue between faith and reason that gave European rationalism a jump-start. Aristotle's philosophy was one thing, but what Ibn Rushd and others gave Europe was Semitic religion's response to Greek reason. It helped thinkers on both sides of the issue deal with the perplexing and disturbing new message that was coming to them from the Islamic world.

That message was simply this: humans had the power. They had the power to glean the laws of the eternal universe by observing their effects in the physical world. And though individual souls might perish with the body, we would merge at death with the one soul that linked together the whole chain of being.

Naturally the church was horrified. This was a sustained attack against the sacred truths that had defined their society for close to a thousand years. These dangerous ideas had begun to creep into Christendom from newly-conquered Muslim Sicily and Spain, soon penetrating into the universities of Italy and France. The name they gave this philosophical attack was Averroism, its followers godless Arabists, hell-bent on hastening Antichrist's arrival.

One of the staunchest Averroists was Pietro d'Abano, a professor of medicine and philosophy who eventually came to the University of Padua in 1306. So revered was he that one of his students, when arriving at d'Abano's lecture hall cried out, "Hail, O Holy Temple!"

Padua was soon branded a college of heretics, with d'Abano at its head. Defying the decrees of the church, he brought Aristotle and Ibn Rushd into the university curriculum. Students would now be instructed in natural philosophy, which he claimed should be the new basis of science. Following the thoughts of al-Razi, Ibn Sina and Ibn Rushd, d'Abano articulated with others a new concept in Europe that was perhaps Islam's greatest contribution to the world: the scientific method. Tradition and the Bible were no longer adequate methods for discovering truth. Observation, experimentation and logic were the new tools of the trade. It seemed as if d'Abano and his students were on the verge of a brave, new world. But the Inquisition had other plans.

Formed by the church to combat heresy—and shatter the Averroist movement—the Inquisition condemned d'Abano for violating Catholic doctrine in fifty-five separate passages of his books. He died in 1315, before he could be brought to trial. But that didn't stop the Inquisition. They found him guilty anyway, and ordered his dead body to be burned at the stake. According to tradition, his loyal students hid d'Abano's remains, so the church had to make do with burning him in effigy.

At any rate, it was too late. One of d'Abano's students, Dante Alighieri, understood how valuable the contributions of Islamic philosophy were to the new movement, which became known as the Renaissance. In a rare fit of sensitivity, the poet consigned Ibn Sina and Ibn Rushd to Limbo rather than Hell, where they joined the other great philosophers who had the misfortune of being born before Jesus. Saint Thomas Aquinas, quoting extensively from Ibn Rushd and Ibn Sina, tried to do what al-Kindi had done before him—effect a harmony between his faith and the new philosophy. Known as scholasticism, Aquinas's system became both official Catholic doctrine as well as, in a sense, the requiem of the Middle Ages. In 1512, a Lateran Council condemned the philosophy of Ibn Rushd and declared anyone who professed it a heretic and infidel. But whether the church wanted to admit it or not, Averroism—the legacy of Islamic philosophy—had become a part of the European heritage, leading it into the future, into the uncharted territory of the modern world.

7

A Medieval War on Terror

In the Middle Ages, Christendom was completely surrounded by Islam. Asia, Africa and even parts of Europe were controlled by Muslims. For most Christians it mattered little. Many even enriched themselves by trading with their religious rivals. But for the theologians, Islam's dominance was a sorry state of affairs. Not surprisingly these religious men painted a bleak picture of the "infidel." If one considers that Christian monks were the only historians of the Middle Ages, it becomes obvious why Muslims time and again got the worst of press.

Take the *Song of Roland*, the French national epic. This lusty poem of sword-play and self-sacrifice was loosely—very loosely— based on Charlemagne's campaign in Northern Spain in 770. After a very unsatisfactory showing, the Frankish knights beat a hasty retreat across the Pyrenees. Their rear guard was attacked and Roland, Frankish knight par excellence, let himself and his men be cut to ribbons to save the imperial entourage. Strangely, the poet substitutes Muslims for the Christian Basques who actually inflicted the damage.

While lavishing invective on Roland's foes, the author manages to display a startling ignorance of Muslims and their religion. In his desire to portray them as the dark side to Christianity the poet has Muslims worship a trinity comprising Apollo, Muhammad and "Tervagen." He also refers to statuary these "pagan" idol worshippers use in their demonic rituals.

These charges of polytheism and idol-worship are all the more amusing when one considers that the fundamental statement of Islamic faith is that there is no god but God (the one God) and that the Qur'an prohibits the use of images of any kind in worship. Looking at the medieval Christians on the other hand we find them worshipping not just God but his Son as well as his Spirit and his Mother. On top of that, any Muslim going into a church at the time would have no doubt been surprised by the abundant supply of images—or, one might say, *idols*—of Christ, the Virgin, and the saints, not to mention the holy relics venerated for their divine healing powers.

Even if he despises them for their religion, *Roland's* creator does invest a few Muslims with some redeeming qualities like bravery and swordsmanship. Their superior wealth and culture is alluded to, albeit obliquely, in the descriptions of their magnificent garments, armor and weapons. But however admirable the enemy might be the very best the Franks can say of a Muslim is: "God, what a lord, if he were but a Christian!"

Why would the Franks go to such lengths to malign Muslims? Why rewrite history?

The clue is in the date of composition, somewhere around the 1090s. It just so happens that in that decade a group of religious fundamentalists began preaching a holy war against the world's great empire. These barbarians resented the empire's superior culture, scientific know-how and open-minded religion. In fact, the fanatics hated their whole way of life. A few of their most radical clerics organized an army of terrorists to attack the empire at one of its holiest places. They took the citizens of the empire by surprise, massacring thousands upon thousands in an insane bloodbath. The empire had little choice but to wage war in defense of civilization.

Very little differs between then and now except who is on the receiving end. This is the ugly cycle of prejudice, ignorance and death that Europeans began in the Crusades.

GOOD VS. EVIL

If there was any one thing that got me interested in history and in the Middle Ages in particular, it was a book I found in my middle school library when I was twelve years old. It was titled *The Crusades* by Anthony West and told the story of the First Crusade to "rescue the Holy Land from the Moslems." I can still vividly recall the line drawings of mustachioed knights hacking up turbaned riders as well as the lurid descriptions of dismemberment and decapitation of the captured "Saracens." Without having any idea exactly who these Saracens were, I was made to know that they didn't belong in the "Holy Land." We Western Christians had a claim on that sacred piece of real estate because Jesus walked there a thousand years before. This "warrior people" had somehow gotten possession of the Holy Land and, worst of all, Jerusalem. They were making it very hard on the pilgrims and other poor Christians who still lived there. Somehow these Saracens had to be stopped!

West's book ushered me into an era where great deeds were still possible, a comic book world where heroes and villains really lived. Here God gave people victory over their enemies in battle and men killed other men with the best of intentions—to send to hell people who should already be there anyway. History was *The Lord of the Rings* and we were the men, while the "Saracens" were the Orcs. I imagined myself as one of the Frankish knights, traveling half-way across the world to fight the good fight, the just war. This history-as-epic made fantasy appear real.

The operative word however is "appear," for most Western histories of the Crusades are far more fiction than fact. Insanely biased, culturally and religiously, accounts such as the one I read continue to fuel the flames of hatred among Christians and Muslims today. Medieval history is not just the dusty accounts of dead men. It has become a living blueprint to conduct new wars of terror. After the horrific events of September 11, 2001, George W. Bush preached a new "crusade." He did not use the term lightly. All who listened knew what the Crusades were about: light versus dark, in more ways than one.

How strange that it is not the cultural interactions of the Italian republics with Islam, nor Europe's acceptance of the revolutionary Averroist philosophy, nor its genesis as a civilized region thanks to Muslim medicine, science and mathematics that makes the history books. There is only one encounter between Europe and the Islamic world worthy of mention: the Crusades, in all their fundamentalist glory.

Thankfully, in recent years some revisionists have begun to dismantle the saintly aura surrounding these wars of terroristic aggression. But for the majority, the general theme of the book I read years ago holds true: Muslims are always the aggressors. Their life is fundamentally different from ours. Their religion is a false one, of no relationship to the "Judeo-Christian heritage." Most importantly, their terrifying jihads are always somehow less justified than our self-righteous crusades.

These falsehoods, made truths through the warped lens of ignorance and bigotry, all got their start in 1096, though the events which led to the Crusades began many years before.

THE GREAT SCHISM OF ISLAM

Byzantium, the lone Christian stronghold in the East, was a perennial target of Muslim armies. With their control over the Bosphorus, the gateway to the Mediterranean, the Byzantines held a precious prize that they would defend not just against Muslims but Europeans as well. Over the centuries Byzantium had shrunk from a major empire to a minor regional power. Muslim armies hammered against Constantinople like a ceaseless tide. Each year more and more of the Greek kingdom slipped away to join the Muslim ocean. By the tenth century, it looked as if Byzantium would soon become extinct.

Then came a revolution from within Islam. By the time it was over, the entire Muslim world was in a shambles. Soon a power vacuum opened wide enough to let in the Crusaders, scavengers preying on a great empire weakened by schism.

Like Western Christianity, Islam is no stranger to division. A wealth of sects and doctrinal differences still divide the Muslim world today. But no difference of opinion was more tumultuous than that between Sunnis and a new kind of Muslim—the Shia.

Shiaism began as a political protest against the Umayyad caliphate. What was first a movement of Arabs against caliphs not related to the prophet soon embraced Persians, dissatisfied with the racist Umayyads, who did their best to bar Persians from higher positions of power.

After the Umayyads were dispatched, the Abbasid caliphate went on to create a Pax Islamica that spread from Central Asia to the Atlantic ocean. A plethora of ethnic groups was absorbed into the empire. Many of these groups, especially the Persians and the Berbers, rankled at their second-class status. Even within the Arab elite, a new social class of artisans and merchants increasingly grew to resent the spendthrift ways of the aristocracy.

To these various excluded groups, the new sect of Shiaism was a welcome alternative to orthodox Sunnism. A millenial religion, Shiaism promised the return of a spiritual leader known as the Mahdi, descended from Ali, nephew and son-in-law of the Prophet and rightful leader of Islam. With the Imam's return, the lost purity of Islam will be restored, reconciling all classes and races. This new Imam was not a simple religious leader but was divinely guided and thus infallible. The Qur'an was not to be taken literally but had a hidden, symbolic meaning that was open only to the initiated. While Sunni Islam helped to reinforce the social hierarchy of the Abbasids, Shiaism was an egalitarian sect, appealing to outcasts and the disenfranchised, much as Christianity had done centuries before.

The new doctrine was quick to spread. *Da'is*, or missionaries, spread the word of the hidden Imams, whose identities remain shrouded in secrecy to this day. Organized in cells that spanned the entire caliphate, the Shias were a religious underground frequently encountering suppression and execution, once again mirroring the experience of early Christians. While fragmenting the unity of Islam, Shiaism itself would fall victim to schism. In later years two major sects emerged: the Twelvers and the Seveners, so called for their disagreement over the succession of imams.

These religious differences, however, did little to dilute the power of their message. In 893, a Yemenite named Abu Abdallah al-Shi'i converted the Berbers to Shiaism. An ethnic underclass in Arab-dominated North Africa, the Berbers were ferocious fighters and passionate converts. With a joint Shia army of disaffected Arabs and Berbers, Abu Abdallah conquered a series of Arab principates in Northern Africa and proclaimed his new kingdom to be the true caliphate in 909. This new dynastic family, known as the Fatimids, would rule Egypt for the next two hundred and fifty years.

The effect of the rise of the Fatimids was earth-shattering. For the first time in centuries, the authority of the Abbasid caliphs was challenged and a new sect claimed the loyalty of all Islam. Unlike the Sunnis, however, these Fatimids believed in an Imam who was the infallible and sinless representative of Allah himself.

Islam as a unified world empire was over.

Caligula, Fatimid Style

By the middle of the tenth century, the Fatimids were reaching their high tide. Conquering all of Northern Africa by 973, they were poised to extinguish the Abbasids once and for all. Three groups frustrated their plans. The Abbasid lands had fallen into the hands of Shia Buyids, natives of Persia. Meanwhile the Karmathians (a radical group of Shias who had sacked Mecca and even stolen the stone of the Ka'ba) had grown disenchanted with their less extreme cousins to the west and had attacked Fatimid armies in Syria, checking their advance into Iraq. At the same time, the Byzantines had taken advantage of the chaos in the Muslim world to begin reconquering some of their ancient holdings.

There were disturbing events on the domestic front as well, all centered around the new caliph, al-Hakim. Inheriting the throne in 996 at the age of eleven, al-Hakim would go on to distinguish himself as one of the most bizarre figures in Islamic history.

At the tender age of fifteen he executed the eunuch who had ruled in his stead as regent. Al-Hakim then proceeded to pass a series of repressive and arbitrary laws. Trade during the day was abolished. Only during the night hours could business go on. Drinking and gambling were made illegal. Dogs and women were forbidden from appearing in public, the former being slain on sight. He even went to the extraordinary length of outlawing the manufacture of women's shoes, to keep the females at home, barefoot and pregnant. The caliph himself would roam the streets at night, making sure his decrees were enforced. Violators could expect a swift decapitation.

A reign of terror ensued for Muslims, Christians and Jews alike. The People of the Book were forced to wear specific clothes that identified their religion. Numerous laws were passed to restrict their freedoms and humiliate their dignity. Their churches and synagogues were destroyed, including the Church of the Resurrection in Jerusalem.

The caliphal court became witness to a Stalinesque purge. Everyone was suspect and paranoia reigned. The mad caliph saw to it that high ranking soldiers and courtiers lived in fear. One general was executed after reportedly witnessing al-Hakim dismember a child's corpse.

The people could tolerate only so much. The last straw arrived in the person of two da'is from Persia, one of whom was named Darazi. This sage proclaimed that the spirit of God that had been incarnate in Ali and all the other imams was now present in al-Hakim himself. Not surprisingly, al-Hakim was enthusiastic about being proclaimed a near-deity, though he did not publicly support Darazi.

In 1021, al-Hakim went for one of his midnight rambles in the desert and never returned. Although the caliph was most likely the victim of conspiracy, Darazi continued to proclaim al-Hakim as the Mahdi, Shiaism's messianic figure, and the cult of the Druzes to this day awaits al-Hakim's apocalyptic return. Hopefully he will take his time.

His successor tried to undo the damage, rebuilding the Christian places of worship and normalizing relations between the three faiths. Yet despite the fact that Muslims continued to treat Christians and Jews with far more tolerance and equanimity than anywhere else in the medieval world, the repercussions of al-Hakim's madness reached far and wide. By harassing Christian pilgrims and burning their churches, he had provided an unfortunate pretext for holy war.

THE SELJUKS

Throughout the Shia Revolution, the Abbasid caliphs had been relying increasingly on the services of mercenaries from the East. These were the Turks, a newly converted group of Central Asian tribes. They soon overcame their Persian overlords and overran kingdoms in Khurasan and Transoxiana (near the Aral Sea). What made them especially attractive to the Abbasids was their adherence to Sunni Islam. As Sunnis they supported the Abbasid rulers as the rightful leaders of Islam and would stand with them against the Shia Fatimids of Egypt.

In the 1050s, just forty years before the First Crusade, Fatimids and Turks squared off. Each side supported its own caliph for the ancient throne in Baghdad. Thanks to the Seljuks, a tribe of Turkish warriors, the Abbasids successfully regained the throne in 1060. Sunni Islam was saved and the Fatimids had reached their high water mark. From now on they would have to be content with Egypt and its environs.

The caliphate as a political power, however, was over. The Abbasids ruled in name only with the Seljuks now running the show.

Tughril, their leader, took the title Sultan, the Commander of the Faithful, pledging to defend Islam against schism and attack.

Most of the Arabs and Persians were not impressed. They saw the Seljuks as uncouth barbarians. Worse, these Turks brought other Central Asian tribesmen along who were even less disciplined, making war with the indigenous Bedouin and Kurdish nomads. To relieve some of the internal pressure, the Seljuks decided to attack the Byzantines, whose power was in serious decline.

The result was the Battle of Manzikert in 1071, where the Seljuks defeated a combined army of Byzantines and their less than enthusiastic Norman and Turkish soldiers-for-hire. It was a cataclysmic defeat, made even worse by the unprecedented and humiliating capture of the Byzantine Emperor himself. Nearly all of Asia Minor was now in Muslim hands. Nothing was left of the once-magnificent empire of the East except its capital city of Constantinople and a sliver of coastline.

The Emperor paid his ransom and returned to the remnants of his kingdom. It was there that he composed a pitiful plea to the pontiff of Rome, begging for aid. That was when the trouble really started.

The Pope vs. the Kings

The Battle of Manzikert was the high point of the Seljuk sultanate. Soon afterwards, they lost any centralized power they had acquired. In the ensuing chaos a host of would-be sultans began fighting among themselves for supremacy. The Abbasids, eager to regain their lost prestige, played the Turks against each other, weakening all sides. At the same time, the Fatimids of Egypt had lost the Maghrib, all of Islamic Northern Africa, to the Berbers. Deprived of their revenues to the West, the Fatimids took advantage of the instability of the Seljuk regime to invade Palestine and Syria.

It was at this precise moment, when the Islamic world was at its most divided and weakened state in history, that a horde of barbarians and religious fanatics from the West touched down at Constantinople and made their way for Jerusalem, broadswords in hand.

There was no special reason for Western Christians to help their Eastern brethren. The Pope and the Byzantine Patriarch had parted ways in 1054 in the mother of all falling-outs, the Great Schism. The catholic and apostolic church split into two halves, eastern and western, with no love lost between. After all of this, the Pope most likely thought the Byzantine loss at Manzikert was well-deserved.

But the Pontiff was also astute enough to notice the amazing string of Christian victories against Muslim armies. First a Muslim navy had been driven from its base in Provence in 927, and then Pisa and Genoa had reconquered Sardinia in 1016. Christians had made inroads into al-Andalus, seizing possession of Toledo, which soon became the new capital of Catholic Spain. And just a few years before, in 1091, the Normans had conquered Muslim Sicily. The internal pressures of the Shia schism and the Fatimid challenge to the Abbasids had weakened Islam's hold. Now Byzantium itself was at death's door. There was a power vacuum yawning in Palestine and Asia Minor. Why not take the opportunity to extend the boundaries (and revenues) of the Catholic Church by a few thousand miles? Perhaps they might even deal a death blow to Islam. With victory after victory in the West, the Christians did seem to finally have the upper hand.

But Constantinople and Jerusalem were distant objectives. What the Pope was most interested in was Europe and the growing power of kings. For most of the Middle Ages, the West had lacked any central authority, with petty warlords and their thugs squabbling with each other for a few scraps of land. Over the past century, however, things had changed. The warlords were bullied into submission by bigger warlords who called themselves kings. With more land and money at their disposal than ever before, these upstarts began to challenge the one authority that had ruled Europe since the fall of Rome: the church. Kings began to appoint bishops of their choosing, bypassing the church completely and funneling the subsequent tithes into their own pockets.

What was in fact happening was the slow evolution of European society toward absolutism, the creation of nations organized under a centralized monarchy. That kind of power was anathema to the church, long used to controlling the political arena. The Popes thus began to stir up trouble with the lesser nobles, urging them to rebel against the Holy Roman Emperor and other kings who had managed to accumulate too much control to suit Rome. The monarchs eventually got the message and backed off. But now the die was cast. It was to be a contest between Pope and kings with Europe itself as the prize.

The Crusades came at this crucial time, giving the church the opportunity it needed to win the hearts and minds of Europeans from their kings. It united Europe as a cultural entity. That collective identity was not national or ethnic. It was religious, a creation of the church. Now the supreme spiritual leader set about proving his temporal mettle by doing what no king could even dream of: mobilizing an army 150,000 strong to march across the world and fight on his command, while at the same time cowing monarchs into leading the expedition. The Crusades would keep the kings diverted for centuries and drain their coffers while the church maintained its hold on Europe's intellectual, cultural and spiritual life as well as its revenues and land.

THE FRANKS ARE COMING

Of course this would not be the best way to word it to a gullible populace. Without wasting any time, Pope Urban II and his emissaries went on a speaking tour through France to drum up recruits. Peter the Hermit was one of the most accomplished rabble rousers. What he and others all over Europe told the assembled masses was this: Kill the enemies of the faith and all of your sins will be forgiven. Who could pass up such an opportunity?

In March of 1096, Peter led an army of about 10,000 soldiers of God with a large number of camp followers all eager to see where

Christ walked. This was known as the Peasants' Crusade, only the first in a series of successive waves of European invasions of the Middle East. The name, however, is a misnomer. The leaders were no peasants but noblemen, albeit ones fallen on hard times. Their money and supplies ran out by the time they got to Hungary. When they began looting and pillaging to feed themselves, the Magyars gathered an army and decimated their forces in several battles. Peter and his cohorts scrambled out of Hungary and made it to Constantinople, much worse for wear.

When they presented themselves at the Byzantine capital, the Emperor was not impressed. This was not so much a professional army as a riotous mob of uncouth barbarians, thousands strong. The Byzantines hastily ferried them to Asia Minor. After hysterically slaughtering the dark-skinned locals there—who happened to be Christian—the hapless Crusaders were promptly cut to ribbons by the Seljuks.

Meanwhile in Germany, the redoubtable Count Emich of Leiningen was getting his crusade off to a good start. The Count believed himself to be a legendary figure of the Apocalypse. After defeating Antichrist, Count Emich hoped to be crowned King of the World in Jersualem and usher in a thousand-year kingdom.

While he was on his way through the Rhineland the Count decided that the best way to begin his crusade would be to kill every Jew he and his army could lay their hands on. After all, why wait to kill Muslims when the murderers of Christ were right under their noses?

From town to town, the Crusaders spread like a pestilence, giving the inhabitants the choice of conversion or death. Many chose to die, some families even committing suicide rather than give the Christians the satisfaction of killing them. Torah scrolls were burned and synagogues savaged. Sometimes the killing was economically motivated. By killing the Jewish money-lenders who financed their armies, the Crusaders could sail away, debt-free.

From now on, time and again, Crusaders would start off their journeys with similar pogroms. It was the beginning of European anti-

Semitism, a loathsome by-product of Christian fanaticism and holy war that would haunt the world for centuries to come.

BLOODBATH IN JERUSALEM

More seasoned and professional soldiers were also making their way to Palestine. This was the grand army of Crusaders led by a series of Norman and Frankish noblemen and adventurers, including Count Bohemund of Taranto, his brother Tancred, and Godfrey de Bouillon, who would become the first king of the new Christian kingdom of Jerusalem.

They arrived at the perfect time. The Muslim world was in a shambles. Shiaism was fatally divided, with the waning Fatimids now facing off against the Assassins, a radical Ismaili Shia sect with strongholds in Persia and Syria. In what was left of the caliphate, the Sunni Abbasids played one Seljuk against another, hoping to weaken them all and regain their long-lost control. At the same time, regardless of creed, Turks, Arabs and Kurds went on killing each other for what was left of the once mighty Islamic Empire.

By 1098 the Crusaders had scored a series of surprise victories against the Turks. Capitalizing on Muslim disunity, the Europeans managed to undo a great deal of the damage done at Manzikert. From Nicea to Edessa, the triumphant forces of Christendom were crying, "Deus hoc vult!" or "God wills it!" Religious euphoria aside, the petty noblemen of Europe were ecstatic. Here were kingdoms for the taking. Each began to carve out his territory, even killing local Christian rulers to stake their claim more forcefully.

There was nothing to stand in their way—especially after a traitor at Antioch helped them to take the recalcitrant city after a long siege. By the time they got to the walls of Jerusalem, the emotions of the Crusaders were at a fever pitch. God, they were convinced, had been behind all their victories. Weeping with awe, they surged into the city on July 15, 1099. It was then, with cries of "God wills it!" that the real horror began.

In a two-day long orgy of murder, the crazed victors slaughtered every Muslim and Jew in the city, including children and infants. As eye-witness Raymond d'Aguilers put it:

> Wonderful sights were to be seen. Some of our men (and this was more merciful) cut off the heads of their enemies; others shot them with arrows, so that they fell from the towers; others tortured them longer by casting them into the flames. Piles of heads, hands and feet were to be seen in the streets of the city. It was necessary to pick one's way over the bodies of men and horses. But these were small matters…in the Temple and porch of Solomon, men rode in blood up to their knees and bridle reins. Indeed it was a just and splendid judgment of God that this place should be filled with the blood of the unbelievers since it had suffered so long from their blasphemies.

It was also reported that the Franks "boiled Pagan adults in cooking pots," as a chronicler put it. "Not only did our troops not shrink from eating dead Turks and Saracens, they also ate dogs."

What did the Crusaders see when they pulled Muslim and Jewish children from their parents and bashed their brains out? Did they see human beings? It seems unlikely. The Crusaders were living the Apocalypse, after all. These cowering creatures before them were the minions of Antichrist. They were not people made in God's image but filthy monsters, less than human, who could be exterminated like so many vermin. All in the name of the Prince of Peace.

No one knows exactly how many perished in this horrifying atrocity. By the end of the bloodbath, Jerusalem's native inhabitants were completely annihilated. A conservative estimate of the death toll is forty thousand men, women and children—after only two days. For comparison, it is a little bit less than all the Americans who died in Vietnam over a ten year period.

When the few survivors arrived in Baghdad after a torturous journey, their pitiful story was greeted with disbelief and then apathy. Jerusalem was a long way off, a backwater to the urbane citizens of the ancient capital. More, it had belonged to the Fatimids, who had only a few years before won it from the Seljuks. No doubt the caliph was more than happy to see his rivals get their come-uppance, and at the hands of barbarians no less. Besides, there were more pressing problems to the East, where the heart of the Seljuk sultanate had fallen to a pagan army from Central Asia. The Crusaders were indeed an annoyance, but they did after all only occupy a tiny sliver of coastline in Syria. Jerusalem would just have to wait.

Of course, to many Muslims this felt like a betrayal. One religious leader led the survivors of Jerusalem through Baghdad, crying, "I see the supporters of the faith are weak!" But the guilt trip didn't work. No one cared. While the Crusaders called all Muslims "Saracens" and made no distinction between them, the followers of the Prophet—Fatimids, Shias, Seljuks and Abbasids were woefully divided. Islam had become its own worst enemy.

Jihad

There were now four Crusader states stretching from Asia Minor to the edge of the Red Sea: the Duchy of Edessa, the Principality of Antioch, the County of Tripoli and the Kingdom of Jerusalem. They were islands of European Christian feudalism in a sea of Islam, having as little cultural contact with their enemies as possible. For decades they were left unmolested.

Then in November 1144, the Turkish general Zengi set off on a campaign to take Damascus from its Arab amir. The Duchy of Edessa happened to be along the way and Zengi besieged it, to get his troops primed for the assault on Syria. To his surprise the Christian city quickly fell. Suddenly Islam had a new hero. The refugees from Jerusalem began to pack their bags.

Their hopes were shattered when Zengi was assassinated two years later by one of his eunuchs, a Frank. But his son Nur al-Din picked up the cause and declared a jihad to defend Islam against the barbarian invaders and unite the caliphate once again.

Jihad means struggle in Arabic. It does not mean holy war. This "struggle" simply means striving to be a better Muslim. Contrary to popular conception, Islam is no more a religion of aggression than is Christianity. Indeed, the Qur'an seems tame compared to the Bible, which in certain verses condones genocide (Leviticus 26:7-9, Numbers 33:52-53, 55, I Samuel 15:18, and just about the whole book of Joshua). People of all religions have a habit of misinterpreting sacred texts to justify practically anything, no matter how horrible.

Like the Bible, however, the Qur'an is more concerned with social justice and faith in God than condoning war or strife. Nevertheless the Qur'an does allow Muslims to take up arms in defense of their faith and their homes. Strange as it may have seemed to the Crusaders, Muslims had lived in and governed the "Holy Land" for four hundred years—longer than any Christian power. This was their home.

Moreover, in all that time the Muslims had coexisted with Christians and Jews within their domains, as the Qur'an commanded them. Aside from the madness of al-Hakim, Christians, Jews and Muslims lived together in Jerusalem in a culture of relative tolerance unknown in Christendom.

That harmony was shattered by the savage fanaticism of the Franks at Jerusalem. War was no longer to be a civilized contest to steal someone's land or money. Its honest albeit immoral motives were now to be masked by wretched superstition, cultural arrogance and genocidal frenzy. If this was what Western Christianity looked like, the Muslims had seen enough. A new war of liberation began to free their homeland from the foreign invader.

The Empire Strikes Back

For every action there is an equal or greater reaction. The name of this particular reaction was Salah al-Din, the greatest hero of medieval Islam. His biographer Baha al-Din described him as the pinnacle of Islamic manhood: an honest and pleasant companion, a defender of orphans and the elderly, and a mighty warrior well-versed in the Qur'an, history, poetry and even the genealogy of Arabian horses! More than anything, he was a *mujahid*, a warrior fighting to liberate his people from oppression. When one of his companions once asked him, "What is the most noble death?" Salah al-Din replied, "Death in God's path. Well, then, the worst that can befall me is the most noble of deaths!"

He was born in 1138 to a Kurdish family in Iraq. His uncle Shirkuh was Nur al-Din's trusted friend and a general in his army. In 1164 a faction within the weakened Fatimid state asked Nur al-Din for help against their opponents who had, amazingly, signed a treaty with the Franks. Shirkuh was sent with a two-fold mission: expel the Crusaders and make Egypt a Seljuk satellite. Shirkuh took along his young nephew, who was more interested in partying than exercising his sword arm.

In 1167 Salah got his first taste of battle. Ordered by his uncle to take Alexandria, the first-time commander did an admirable job, but could not prevail against the superior artillery and naval power of the Crusaders. He withdrew to Cairo, where Shirkuh made himself vizier, reigning in the place of the Fatimid caliph, who was still a child. Then in 1169, Shirkuh died. Nur al-Din would follow five years later leaving the way open for Salah al-Din to rule supreme in the Islamic heartland.

After two years of consolidating his power, mainly by replacing the highly-suspect Fatimid army with his own force of fellow Kurds, Syrians and Sunni Egyptians, Salah al-Din decided to dissolve the Fatimid caliphate. For the first time in hundreds of years, the name of the Caliph of Baghdad was inserted in the Friday prayers. It was a bloodless revolution that brought relief to the predominantly Sunni Egyptians, who had always looked at the Fatimids as invaders and heretics.

Salah al-Din had changed in the past few years. Transformed from a thoughtful but pleasure-loving youth, he became convinced that God had elevated him from obscurity to unify Islam and rid its lands of the barbarian Crusaders. His rapid rise to power had not corrupted him. Instead he lived humbly, distributed lavish alms to the poor and avidly studied the Qur'an and the Hadith. Listening to the words of Scripture, his eyes would fill with tears. Islam had fallen low, a victim of its own sins. But no longer. Salah al-Din vowed to wipe out the Crusaders, to "destroy the last one on the surface of the earth of those who do not believe in Allah—or else I die."

Not all were prepared to follow where he led. The Shia Assassins remained bitter enemies of the Sunni leader. They even joined a bizarre alliance of Latin Kingdom Franks and Normans from Sicily to attack Alexandria by sea. These strange bedfellows were eventually beaten back. After surviving two assassination attempts, Salah al-Din went on the offensive against the Shias, but was unable to breach the walls of their impregnable fortress.

It was no great loss. The Assassins were, after all, never more than a nuisance. A bigger prize lay within his reach. After a long campaign, Salah al-Din conquered Syria and thus brought the ancient heartland of Islam under the caliph's banner. All that remained was Palestine and its holy city Jerusalem, where Muhammad ascended to heaven in his visionary Mir'aj. It would take a devoted army of mujahadeen to liberate Jerusalem and restore the muezzin's call to its hallowed walls. The Crusaders were about to learn a lesson Jesus once taught: "As ye sow, so shall ye reap."

The two armies, after many battles, met on the slopes of Hittin in 1187 for the endgame. According to tradition, it was here that Jesus preached his Sermon on the Mount. It was the evening of Qadr, the anniversary of Muhammad's first revelation from Allah. Salah al-Din's forces prayed and sang to commemorate this holiest of nights. Surely, they thought, the date was no coincidence.

When dawn broke, with cries of "Allahu akbar!" the Muslims attacked. The mujahadeen destroyed the Frankish troops, who were already half-dying of thirst from the long desert march. Many of the Franks rushed toward the nearby Sea of Galilee, where Jesus had appeared to his disciples walking on the water. But the water was fatally out of reach. By the afternoon the Christians were cut to ribbons, blood blotting out the sight of their lost Holy Land. The Crusader Kingdom of Jerusalem was no more. Victory assured, Salah al-Din dismounted and wept with joy as he offered a prayer of thanks to God.

The King himself had been taken captive, along with several Frankish noblemen. One of them was Reynauld of Chautillon, who years before had massacred a caravan of pilgrims on their way to Mecca. Worse, he had attacked Medina, Muhammad's resting place and even planned to assault Mecca itself.

Salah al-Din took out his scimitar, sliced Reynauld's head off his neck and dragged the corpse through the dust to the former king of Jerusalem. This, he told the king, was for Reynauld's crimes. The others, however, would be held captive for a time and then released. The Muslims fought a different kind of holy war, one that did not involve senseless slaughter. No quarter was given only to those knights who belonged to religious orders—the Templars and Hospitallers. To Salah al-Din these warrior-monks were a lethal combination of brutality and fanaticism. He looked on approvingly as they were executed one by one. As the last one perished, so did any European hope of empire in the "Holy Land." At least for seven hundred years or so.

THE SEQUELS

Of course the story doesn't end there. More Crusades were fought, with all-star casts including Holy Roman Emperors, Kings of France, and Robin Hood's favorite monarch, Richard the Lionheart. None of these men were able to do what the First Crusade had accomplished through fortune and faith.

The church, frustrated in its designs on the Middle East, was forced to attack the pagan Slavs and Prussians, French heretics and stubborn Italian Catholics who resented the Pope's authority. New campaigns began in Spain to pay tit for tat. By the end of the fifteenth century, al-Andalus was lost forever and Ferdinand and Isabella, after expelling the Jews, were free to send Columbus to exploit, enslave and ultimately exterminate the hapless people of the Caribbean.

What had the Crusaders accomplished? The eminent medievalist Steven Runciman put it best: "The Crusades were launched to save Eastern Christendom from the Moslems. When they ended the whole of Eastern Christendom was under Moslem rule."

In the end, the Crusades were a failure. Christianity failed, the Papacy failed, and European ambition failed. While the Reconquista of Spain seemed to balance the scales, the Ottoman Turks had already overrun most of the Balkans a hundred years earlier. Just a few decades before, in 1453, the Turks had conquered Constantinople. The ancient capital of Eastern Christendom was known by a new name—Istanbul—and still is today. Within a hundred years Muslims would occupy Hungary and control it till the eighteenth century, invading Austria as late as 1683. Despite the best efforts of the church, a Muslim nation has existed in one part of Europe or another since 711 AD.

So how to understand the enduring fascination with the Crusades? Why has so much ink been spilled over this sordid and futile war of religious terror? Perhaps it is all in the myth. Historians over the years have done their best to give the Crusaders a face-lift. In a couple of keystrokes barbarian zealots become cowboys in chainmail, fighting for civilization in a barren desert of turbaned Indians. We can easily convince ourselves that the Muslims are a war-like people, that they are threatening and that they are fundamentally different from us. It is a convenient way to project Western fantasies and anxieties onto the past.

This obsession with Crusades history obfuscates the far more rich and complex cultural interactions between the two civilizations. It stresses difference and aggression over similarities and intellectual advancement. It perpetuates the "us versus them" mentality that is tearing our world apart today.

How often have historians claimed that it was the Crusades that brought Greek wisdom back to Europe? It is a convenient myth for Westerners because it casts them in the active role. They attack the heathens "preserving" their Greek and Roman birthright and reclaim it for those who truly deserve it. But Crusaders couldn't have cared less about philosophy or algebra. They were in Palestine and Syria to enrich themselves with land, serfs and money. The myth then serves as a consolation prize. If the Crusades were a political failure then at least something good came out of them.

It was the memory of the Crusade's failure that weighed on the European consciousness like an albatross. It gave Western culture the mother of all inferiority complexes. Only by asserting its power over the weak and helpless in America, Africa and Asia could Christendom salvage its pride and prestige. The wounds were never completely healed however—not even when the Muslim world was effectively put under Europe's thumb in the nineteenth and twentieth centuries. The old fear remained. It was a fear that dreaded not just the strength of their most implacable rival but worse, the hint of weakness in the Western self.

And now, just as the Crusades were ending, a new war was beginning to erupt. Before modern Europe could be born a titanic struggle would have to be fought, with the fate of civilization hanging in the balance. Out of this terrifying conflict a new world order would emerge, for better or worse.

8

The First World War

A charismatic dictator rising from humble station. A series of
lightning assaults on the surrounding nations, weakened by
division. An attack on Russia in the winter. Europe devastated
by violence. The world's most efficient, ruthless killing machine on the
march. Its goal: world domination.

This is the story of the battle between Mongols and Muslims.

THE CONQUEROR

For most of the Middle Ages, no one had paid much attention to
the Mongols. They were merely one of myriad tribes that periodically
harassed the ailing Chinese empire. Their anonymity ended with the
rise of Temujin (soon to be known as Chingiz Khan) at the turn of the
thirteenth century. Through charisma, ruthlessness and strategy, Chingiz
transformed his tribe of nomadic raiders into the most effective and
brutal army the world had ever seen.

The Mongols didn't spend a lot of time on diplomacy. They
usually sent a curt letter demanding the local lord or king to uncon-
ditionally surrender and kiss the Khan's stirrup. The penalties for
resistance were horrific. Once the Mongols breached the city walls
they burned every building, hunted down men like they were wild

animals, raped every woman and girl in sight, killed whatever infants they wanted and enslaved anyone left standing. Afterwards they might withdraw when the smell of the corpses became too offensive.

Spreading themselves over such a vast distance, the Mongols knew they could never occupy the lands they conquered. They soon learned that if they terrified the populace enough, they wouldn't have to. The people would never dare to rebel when faced with such ferocity. The conquerors could then leave the tax collecting to local lords and roll in from time to time to push people around and take their money. These were people who understood the uses of terror.

Besides being vicious, the Mongols were well-equipped with fire-bombs, smoke screens, siege engines and even gunpowder that made explosions loud enough to terrify an opposing army's horses. Communication between armies in and out of battle was superb, with smoke, semaphores and even swords flashing signals from one end of the field to the next. A rigidly-enforced chain of command from Chingiz himself all the way down to an *arban*, a troop of ten men, prevented any mishaps during a hard day's killing. Battles, campaigns and even skirmishes were planned precisely using detailed maps and intelligence garnered by a host of spies posing as merchants. In short, the Mongols had every advantage over the typical medieval army, Christian or Muslim.

All of these factors helped the Conqueror to make short work of Mongolia and the Turkoman tribes by 1206. With their lands under his thumb and his ranks swelling, he marched on China. In 1215 he breached the Great Wall and captured Beijing. At the city of Chungtu in northern China, Muslim ambassadors witnessed the destruction of the city by fire and sword. They later wrote that the streets were slippery with human fat and cobbled with corpses.

Chingiz's last hurrah was the destruction of Khwarazm, the Muslim ambassadors' homeland. This was the easternmost Muslim kingdom, stretching from Persia to the Hindu Kush mountains of Afghanistan.

Ruled by a series of Turkish warlords, Khwarazm had capitalized on the Silk Road trade. Bukhara, its trading hub, was called the "cupola of Islam," the greatest metropolis in Central Asia.

The Mongol army, a hundred thousand strong, took the city in 1220. After slaughtering the defenders, who gave up in the face of superior numbers, the Mongols turned the largest mosque into a stable, using Qur'an stands as mangers. Ascending the pulpit, Chingiz told the city leaders that he was the punishment of God. Just in case they missed his point, he set fire to the city, killed thirty thousand people and enslaved everyone else.

The fate of Samarqand, the Khwarazmid capital, was no better. Chingiz's terrorism in Bukhara had done its job. Shuddering at the news of that city's destruction, the populace of the capital surrendered after five days. The Mongols quickly separated the people into women who were raped and then enslaved, skilled artisans who were shipped back to toil in Mongolia, and soldiers who were summarily slaughtered. The only people left alive were Muslim and Christian clerics. When the Mongols found the governor they killed him by pouring molten silver into his eyes and ears.

Winding his way back to Mongolia, Chingiz and his army continued to persevere in atrocities. At Nishapur, chroniclers say over a million and a half people were killed. It is most likely an exaggeration but no doubt hundreds of thousands perished during the entire campaign, if not a million total. Grisly pyramids were made out of the heads of victims, one for men, another for women, the last for children. In Balkh, in northern Afghanistan, after killing everyone they could find, the Mongols even slaughtered every chicken, dog, and cat.

Their psychopathic destruction went beyond mere butchery. Most of the Islamic countries were irrigated by a system of underground canals known as *qanats*. These long trenches, which linked a series of wells together, needed to be regularly cleared of accumulated silt. With the population exterminated, the qanats were swallowed up by dirt. Much of Central Asia, which had previously been lush with vegetation, became a barren desert. Without agriculture the once-great cities could sustain only a shadow of their former populations. Khwarazm became a backwater and Islam lost a vast piece of territory. The remnants of the caliphate at Baghdad, on the other hand, still posed a serious challenge to the Mongols. Thus it was decided to turn their attention to a less-civilized and weaker target: Europe.

THE MONGOL INVASION OF EUROPE

By the time word reached the West of Chingiz's exploits, fact was hopelessly garbled by fantasy. For a number of decades, Europeans had been telling tales of Prester John, a Christian king who ruled all of Asia. Numerous letters surfaced, purportedly written by the king himself, which promised to crush the Muslims and regain the Holy Land for the church. As the news of Khwarazm's fall reached Europe, many began to think that Prester John was on the march and Islam would soon be extinct.

It was not all fantasy. Nestorian Christianity had migrated eastward into Turkestan and China. Many of the Mongol soldiers and chieftains were now Christian and every bit as fanatical as the Crusaders. Islam, as the greatest obstacle to Mongol world domination, was indeed slated for destruction. To the church it looked like the hand of God.

Imagine then the Pope's distress on receiving a letter from the King of Hungary in 1223 stating that Mongols had ravaged Russia, slaughtering 200,000 people. That didn't sound like Prester John at all. The Mongols, however, didn't press the issue but withdrew to squabble over control of the empire after Chingiz's death in 1227.

The church breathed a sigh of relief. Surely Prester John had only been targeting the Georgian heretics and not good Catholic folk. Why listen to the Hungarian monarch's dire warning? It was so much easier for Europeans to believe that their most fervid fantasies—the recapture of Jerusalem and the destruction of Islam—were about to become reality.

But the Mongols had other plans. Following Chingiz's death the empire was divided among his sons, with Batu inheriting the westernmost lands. After several years of planning and intelligence gathering, Batu's forces marched on Russia in 1236 and accomplished what Napoleon and Hitler could not: a successful invasion of Russia in the winter. Their first stop after wiping out the Bulgars was Ryazan, in December 1237. Everybody was slaughtered, from the prince and his family to the lowliest peasant. "Some," a chronicler wrote, "were impaled or had nails or splinters of wood driven under their fingernails. Priests were roasted alive and nuns and young girls were raped in the churches in front of their relatives. No eye remained open to weep for the dead."

For the next three years Russia encountered more of the same. By Christmas 1240, Kiev was in Mongol hands. When a papal envoy went through the city six years later, he was still tripping over the skulls and bones of the slaughtered, left to rot where they fell.

Within two years the Mongols were at the threshold of Western Christianity. While most of Europe stuck its collective head in the sand, one king made a valiant attempt to preserve his nation. This was King Bela IV of Hungary, who had inherited a kingdom in shambles, with nobles angling for power and privilege over the once great monarchy. When news arrived at court that the Mongols had entered Hungary, Bela hastily sent his family to Austria, preparing for the worst.

THE BATTLE OF MOHI

By April 10, 1241, the Mongols were camped just outside Pest, having chosen the perfect spot to engage their foe. Just the day before, at the Battle of Leignitz, they had annihilated the main Polish force, using their time-honored tactic of a feigned retreat to lure the Poles into a trap. Nine sacks of ears—one for each victim—were sent to Batu. Now, covered with woods and protected on both sides by rivers, their position was unassailable.

The Hungarians bivouaced on the heath of Mohi, an open plain at a little distance from the Sajo that commanded a panoramic view. Nevertheless, the king decided to encircle the camp with a barricade of wagons, to ensure against a surprise attack. Bela planned to lure the Mongols on to the right bank of the marshy Sajo, now flooded. A garrison of a thousand knights was detached to guard a stone bridge, the only way to cross the river. The two armies waited for the showdown

It came soon enough. That evening a Russian deserter from the Mongol ranks arrived in the Hungarian camp with the news that the Mongols intended to cross the Sajo that very night. Just before dawn the main Hungarian force arrived at the bridge, ready to check a Mongol advance. After a few volleys of arrows had failed to dent their ranks, the Hungarians began jeering at the Mongols on the other side of the river. At this point Batu began to bombard them with seven catapults he had brought forward in the middle of the night. To the accompaniment of thunderous noise and flashes of fire the Mongols pounded the bridge garrison with stone and fire bombs. It was Europe's first encounter with that fateful concoction, gunpowder. The ensuing din panicked the horses and threw the cavalry into disarray. Batu took advantage of this confusion and advanced under a hail of arrows.

Unknown to the Hungarians, the Mongol army had separated into two main columns—one under Batu at the stone bridge and the other under his second-in-command Subotai, downstream. Subotai had to construct a makeshift bridge out of beams and tree trunks in order to get across the river. These first forays into the Hungarian camp had been nothing but diversions to give him time to complete his mission and surprise the Hungarians from the rear.

As the battle began in earnest, it looked bad for the Mongols. Batu's force took heavy casualties, including thirty of his generals. Without Subotai he was no match for Bela's army. The Hungarians clearly had a superior force, the finest cavalry in Europe, outnumbering the enemy nearly three to one.

After two hours of heavy fighting Batu's army formed a crescent and advanced as if to surround the Hungarians, who charged forward still undaunted, believing that victory was attainable. Just as they began to advance, Subotai surprised them from behind. The Hungarians were now completely surrounded by the Mongol forces. Before the pincers could be closed, they made an orderly retreat into their barricaded camp. Once inside, however, they were decimated by Mongol catapults and firebombs. Soon the Hungarians were in complete disarray. The main body of Mongols rushed upon their camp and pierced its heart, cutting the ropes of the king's tent. His troops fled in panic.

Following close behind, the Mongols spent two days cutting the disorganized Hungarian army to pieces. Using their skills as nomadic hunters, they herded the Hungarians into marshlands and slaughtered them there. Any villages that were foolish enough to give refuge to the survivors were burned to the ground and their inhabitants massacred. For two day's march from the field of Mohi the land was littered with the dead.

Seventy thousand men died at the battle of Mohi or fleeing from it—including Koloman, the King's brother, many bishops and archbishops and most of the Hungarian gentry. The defeat at Mohi was the greatest disaster in the history of Hungary. A Bavarian chronicler wrote, "The Kingdom of Hungary, which began under Emperor Arnulf and has existed for three hundred and fifty years, has been annihilated by the Tartars." The Mongol campaign was just getting warmed up.

On Christmas Day 1241, Batu's troops crossed the frozen Danube to Gran, then the capital of Hungary. By March 1242 their reconnaissance forces had returned from several expeditions into Austria. There was nothing to stand in their way. Schism, greed, and disorganization had weakened Europe. The dagger of the Mongols was poised to deal the coup de grâce.

And then, quite suddenly, a letter arrived from the Mongolian homeland, informing Batu of the death of Ogedei, the supreme ruler of the Mongolian Empire. It was Mongol law that after the death of the Khan, his heirs must return to Mongolia to elect the successor. Reluctantly, Batu abandoned his conquest of Europe for the present and made his way back to the capital of their empire, Karakorum. He would never return. By a twist of fate, Western Europe was spared.

European Aftershocks

Hungary was shattered by the Mongol onslaught. To prevent any invasion in the future, Bela created a system of fortresses. But to keep them manned, he had to dole out vast territories to the nobles. Their power increased while the king's diminished. Eventually Hungary plunged into feudal anarchy and became a holding of the Holy Roman Empire.

The situation was even worse in Russia, where the Mongols remained. State-building was a dim dream for those living under the Mongol yoke. While the rest of Europe was pulling itself out of the Middle Ages, Russia was sinking deeper and deeper into them. Foreign occupation, then as now, caused cultural life to stagnate. Separated from their neighbors to the West, the Russians had to watch from the sidelines while Europe hurtled into the modern world. It was a miserable, humiliating ordeal which set Russia back hundreds of years and forced later dictators like Peter the Great and Josef Stalin to push for an unnaturally rapid modernization, costing countless lives. Death and defeat hung over Eastern Europe heavier than any Iron Curtain. The Mongol invasion had served to split the West in half, isolating those who had absorbed the full impact of war.

Meanwhile the rest of Christendom breathed a sigh of relief and decided, if they could not defeat them, to convert them. That way, the church hoped, they could be used in a final assault on Islam that would wipe the heathen off the face of the earth

Pope Innocent IV sent a diplomatic mission headed by Franciscan monks to parlay with the Great Khan. After a long and arduous journey they came face to face with the potentate himself. There the

Franciscans told him that the Pope requested he be baptized. The Great Khan replied that he was already God's representative on Earth, commanded by God to conquer the world. If the Pope knew what was good for him he would journey to Mongolia and offer his allegiance.

The only good news the monks brought back was that Nestorian Christians were in very high places in the Mongol Empire. Christians in Europe, including King Louis IX, grew a little over-enthusiastic, expecting the Tartars to help them in their newest crusade. Unfortunately for Louis, his hopes were not to be realized. Ignored by the Mongols, Louis was eventually captured and his army destroyed by a new power in Egypt.

These were the Mamluks—Kipchak Turks sold as slaves to the Sultan of Egypt by the Mongols, who used the proceeds to finance their invasion of Europe. Like so many other former nomads, the Mamluks made fierce and cunning warriors. They soon became indispensable to the sultan in combating the fresh wave of Crusaders. But they chafed beneath the weight of their Kurdish masters' arrogance and prejudice. It was during the last official European Crusade of Louis IX that the Mamluks overthrew the Kurdish sultanate and established a military dictatorship. They had five years to consolidate their power before the Mongols came looking for their former slaves.

A new ruler, Mongke Khan, had been elected in Mongolia. Deciding that the conquest of the world must continue at a brisk pace, he charged two commanders with the task. Mongke would take out China's Sung Dynasty with the help of his brother Kubilai (soon to make Marco Polo's acquaintance). Meanwhile Hulegu, another of Mongke's younger brothers, would take the west. There was only one power that stood in their way: the still deeply-fragmented world of Islam. It would be a fight to the death.

The Fall of Baghdad

Hulegu's invasion was the final, and worst, of the Crusades. The Mongol commander hated Islam with a vengeance. This hatred was stoked to fever pitch by Nestorian Christians and Buddhists on his staff. Even more outspoken were his wife and his second-in-command, Kitbuqa, both Christian converts. When the Armenian king had visited Mongke in 1255, the Khan had promised him Jerusalem. Many Eastern Christians subsequently swelled the Mongol ranks, eager to revenge themselves on the Muslims and claim the Holy Land for themselves. Armenians, Georgians and Turks joined with their Mongol commanders to form the most formidable Central Asian army ever to hit the civilized world.

Their first stop was the Assassin's fortress at Alamut. For centuries impregnable, the Shia stronghold had held fast against the likes of Salah al-Din. Now the weak young ruler of their sect had become so terrified of the Mongols that he immediately surrendered. The Mongols proceeded to kill every living thing inside the walls, even the infants. The last ruler of the Assassins was sent to Mongolia where he was kicked to death. For the next two years the remaining Ismailis were ferreted out and completely exterminated. By the time the Mongols were through, the Shias were virtually extinct.

Yet in Baghdad this was good news. The Sunnis were only too happy to see their heretic rivals, so long a destabilizing influence, get their just desserts. The last Abbasid caliph, al-Musta'sim was a weak man given to the pleasures of liquor, harem and "playing with birds." When warned of the Mongol advance he replied that surely they would not begrudge him Baghdad if he handed over the rest of his lands to them. Ibn al-Alkami, his chief minister, urged him not to put up a fight or construct more defenses. At the same time this minister was sending secret messages to the Mongols, urging them to do their worst. While some sources claim it was his Shia faith that made him seek vengeance on the commander of the Sunnis, it is more likely that

Ibn al-Alkami simply desired to make the caliph's palace his own, with the help of his new-found allies.

The Mongols first surrounded the city and began pouring arrows into it. One of the caliph's concubines was singing him a song when an arrow came through the window and killed her on the spot. Suddenly it dawned on the caliph that Baghdad needed defending. He sent 20,000 troops to attack the enemy. When they pitched camp, the Mongols broke the nearby dams. All who were not drowned in the ensuing flood were hacked to a pulp.

On January 30, 1259 Hulegu's forces began to smash the city to pieces. Catapults hurtled palm tree stumps and chunks of demolished masonry. The Mongols penetrated the eastern wall and took the city neighborhood by neighborhood. Seeing his army decimated and his city slowly crumbling away, al-Musta'sim surrendered. Once he arrived at the Mongol camp, Islam's last caliph and his family were wined and dined by Hulegu. Then they were sown up in the finest of carpets and trampled to death.

Baghdad was at the mercy of the Mongols. They hunted down every Muslim they could find, following their usual modus operandi of looting, arson, rape, torture and murder. Many panicked residents fled to the caravanserais and locked themselves in. The Mongols burst through the doors, chased them to the roof and slaughtered them there, till blood was flowing from the gutters to the street. The only ones who were left alone were Jews and Christians, under the orders of Hulegu, and a handful of Shias who had managed to bribe their way to safety.

Many days later those few who had survived emerged from the latrines and sewers that had given them shelter. The Baghdad that they had known, the most glorious city in the world, was gone. The treasures of its libraries, millions of priceless manuscripts, had been burned to a cinder. The mighty palaces and gorgeous mosques were pillaged and demolished. Worst of all, there were the corpses, their stench so rancid that the Mongol forces withdrew with their Georgian and Armenian cohorts. The death toll was perhaps two *million*, with even the most conservative estimates at a staggering 800,000. It was the greatest calamity that had ever befallen the Muslim world, an atrocity beyond comprehension.

With Baghdad fallen, Islam was in danger of becoming extinct. The Mongols would soon overrun the remainder of the Middle East and from there Europe, fulfilling their divine injunction to conquer the world.

AIN JALUT

In 1260, Mongol ambassadors arrived in Cairo. They presented the Mamluk sultan, al-Malik al-Muzaffar Qutuz, with a letter from Hulegu. Arrogantly addressed to "the race of Mamluks who fled before our swords," the letter proclaimed the Mongols "the army of God on His earth....Be warned by the fate of others and hand over your power to us...If you resist you will be destroyed."

Qutuz pondered the odds. The Mongols were perhaps a hundred thousand strong. They had wiped out the Assassins as well as the Abbasids and were presently crushing the Turks in Syria. The Mamluks numbered a paltry twenty thousand and were surrounded by hostile Crusaders and rival Mamluks in Syria, led by the redoubtable Rukn al-Din Baybars al-Bunduqdari. The outlook was grim.

But Qutuz also knew the stakes. The Mamluks could expect no mercy from the Mongols. Cairo would become another Baghdad, a charred, corpse-littered ruin. The Eastern Christians who rode with the Mongols were eagerly anticipating the fall of Palestine and indeed of Islam itself. This was a jihad for the very existence of their faith.

The Mamluk sultan wasted no time. He took the four Mongol envoys to the four corners of the city and had them hacked apart at the waist. Their heads were hung on the city gate. The Mongols had their answer.

Assembling the amirs, who were less than thrilled to be going against the most fearsome army ever created, Qutuz proclaimed a jihad for the cause of God and the defense of the Prophet's religion:

> Amirs of the Muslims! For a long time you have been eating the money of the treasury and now you don't want to fight. I, myself, will set out. He who chooses the jihad will accompany me; he who doesn't can go home. God observes him, and the guilt of those who rape our women will be on the cowards' heads!

To drive his point home, Qutuz rode through the city at night to the beating of drums crying, "I will fight the Tatars by myself!" Seeing that he actually meant it, the shamed amirs began to assemble their armies.

Just as the preparations began, the Muslims were stunned to learn that Hulegu had withdrawn. A continent away, the Great Khan Mongke had died, forcing Hulegu to return to Mongolia. It seemed as if the Mamluks would share in the good fortune that had spared Europe fifteen years before.

But Hulegu was not about to drop his conquest of Islam. Twenty thousand of his troops remained, led by Hulegu's most able commander, Kitbuqa. The Mongol general was a Nestorian Christian and a dire enemy of the Islamic faith. Eager to press on and exterminate the infidel, Kitbuqa advanced into Palestine.

Not all the news that month was bad, however. After Kitbuqa conquered Syria, the rival Mamluk commander Baybars fled with his remaining troops to Cairo, offering his services to Qutuz. Despite an undying enmity between the two—Qutuz had murdered the chieftain of Baybars' tribe—they both understood that a Mongol victory would spell their doom.

There was one last obstacle to hurtle before facing their enemy. The Mamluks would need to pass through the Crusader territory of Acre. In an unprecedented move, Qutuz sent a letter to the Europeans, asking for permission to cross their territory and to buy supplies.

Ever since the Mongol invasion of Europe, Western Christians had had conflicting emotions about the hordes from the East. On one hand, they certainly applauded the destruction of Islam. On the other hand, they realized that their turn was next. While Crusaders may have been inclined to throw in their lot with Hulegu to rid the Middle East of the troubling Mamluks, Pope Alexander IV was vehemently opposed to any such alliances.

The Pope had become appalled by the sudden rise to power of Eastern Christianity. Thanks to the Mongols, the Orthodox Christians were gaining territory in leaps and bounds. Crusaders like Count Bohemund were making alliances with them and even replacing Catholic bishops with Orthodox clergy. Riding with their fearsome allies, the Armenians and Georgians might capture Jerusalem and eclipse the prestige of Western Christendom. It would be a serious propaganda blow.

More than that, the Pope could see—for once—the long-range effects of a Muslim defeat. He realized that no European army could possibly withstand another Mongol assault. If Hulegu's forces overcame the Mamluks, they would march unimpeded all the way to the Atlantic Ocean. The West would go the way of Russia and the church would become extinct.

The handwriting appeared on the wall in 1257. Berke, the younger brother of Batu, had suppressed a Polish and Lithuanian uprising, which had temporarily expelled the Mongols from Volhynia, a Galician city. Berke hit northern Poland like a cyclone, wreaking worse havoc than 1241. Thousands upons thousands were butchered and all the towns and villages, including Krakow, were pillaged and burned to the ground.

Pope Alexander IV begged for Christian aid to Poland. When none came, he preached a crusade against the Mongols but still to no avail. In impotent rage, he excommunicated Count Bohemund for allying himself with the Mongols in Syria. The news reached the Crusader states just as they were deliberating Qutuz's entreaty. Following the Pope's lead, they sided with what was, to them, the lesser of two evils. They sold the Mamluks supplies and let them march unhindered toward their destiny.

Mamluks and Mongols met in Galilee at Ain Jalut, Goliath's Spring. It was here, according to legend, that the shepherd boy David had slain the mighty warrior Goliath. Gathering the amirs together, Qutuz reminded them of what the Mongols had done to Baghdad and what would assuredly happen to their own wives and children. The troops began to weep and vowed once again to defend Islam. But they were still afraid. This was an army that had ravaged the world from China to Austria. It was an army that had annihilated the five hundred year old caliphate and destroyed Islam's greatest city. And it was an army that for sixty years had never been defeated in battle.

Islam's last stand began on September 3, 1260, at sunrise. The Mamluk vanguard under Baybars was the first to advance under thunderous drums. Thinking the entire Mamluk army was before him, Kitbuqa ordered a charge and the two forces collided. Then Baybars played an old Mongol trick, ordering his troops to retreat. The Mongols took the bait and gave pursuit.

Kitbuqa's troops were caught in their own trap. Now the Mamluk force, spread out over a four mile wide area, closed in for the kill. The Mongols, however, were not going to go down so easily. They charged the Muslim flank and ripped it to shreds. From his horse, Qutuz could see the battle was almost lost. He took off his helmet, threw it to the ground and cried, "O Islam!" Then he rode off straight toward the enemy. With cries of "Allahu akbar!" the troops followed, their courage renewed. In the ensuing frenzy, the Muslims killed Kitbuqa, sending the Mongols fleeing in panic. Pursuing them for eight miles, Qutuz's troops hacked the rest to pieces. The sultan dismounted and rubbed his face in the dirt, kissing it. Then he prayed, prostrating himself before the God the Mamluks had fought for that day. David had slain Goliath for a second time.

NEVER TO RETURN

Bearing Kitbuqa's head on a pole, the Mamluks proceeded back to Cairo for a triumphal entry. But along the way, Baybars took his revenge on the man who had murdered the leader of his tribe. During an audience with the victorious sultan, Baybars stabbed him to death and assumed command of the Mamluk army. It was an ignoble end for Qutuz, who had done so much for Egypt and for Islam. Sadly, even the memory of his victory has faded with time.

But the fact remains that in that single victory of the Mamluk army, Islam changed the world and made Europe secure enough from destruction that it could begin to benefit from the other great gift of Islam—knowledge. Ain Jalut belongs with the likes of Marathon and Actium, Hastings and Waterloo, Gettysburg and Stalingrad. Without the victory of Qutuz the Middle Ages would never have ended and the Renaissance would never have begun. It stopped the Mongol conquest of the Western world dead in its tracks. Muslims and Christians, except for those in Russia, would never be menaced by Chingiz's hordes again.

The Mamluks, now the supreme power in the Middle East, conquered the last of the Crusader kingdoms and wreaked a terrible revenge on the Eastern Christians who had sided with their enemies. The Mongols themselves were soon divided by the capable Baybars, who learned that Berke, the leader of the Golden Horde, had converted to Islam. Baybars now began to play his fellow Muslim against Hulegu, Islam's public enemy number one. The two became embroiled in a family feud that lasted until their deaths and fatally weakened the Mongol Empire. By the turn of the century it was in a shambles, broken into a host of separate kingdoms.

While the Mamluk Empire continued to thrive, most of the other areas devastated by the Mongols languished. With their cultural and agricultural life annihilated, Muslims had to build their lives back from scratch. Having felt the full brunt of Mongol ferocity, the lands of Persia and Iraq took years to rebuild. Some communities never recovered. Bubonic plague, arriving a few decades later (courtesy of the Mongols), hit the predominantly urban world of Islam even harder than Europe. One calamity after another kept the heart of Islam devastated and demoralized.

Thanks to Muslim resistance, the West had escaped such all-encompassing destruction. By defeating the Mongols, Muslims had inadvertently given Europe an advantage. With a population safe and sound, cultural institutions intact and Muslim learning revolutionizing their ways of thinking, Europeans were free to begin their quest for the modern world. It is crucial to remember that it was Ain Jalut, more than anything, that saved the rest of Europe from becoming another Russia, mired in feudalism, occupation and cultural stagnation.

But the fallout was even more far-reaching than this. With the Holy Land now firmly in Muslim hands, Christians set their sights on exterminating Islam in Europe. A new crusade began: the Reconquista of Spain. When it was finished, Ferdinand and Isabella had demolished the once glorious culture of al-Andalus, expelling Muslims and Jews alike. The effort, however, nearly bankrupted the Spanish crown.

Trade was the best way to refill the royal coffers. Unfortunately the most lucrative routes were monopolized by the Italian maritime republics. Worse, the Mamluks and Ottoman Turks ran the Eastern Mediterranean tollbooth, demanding heavy duties on all the Silk Road imports going through their bazaars. It was to circumvent the Mamluks and Ottomans that the Spanish monarchs commissioned an Italian sailor from Genoa to find an alternate route. His voyage changed the world and shifted the age-old balance of power. Islam and Christianity would never be the same.

9

Raiders of
The Lost Library

Throughout the Middle Ages, Islam and Christendom were in constant interaction, even during the Mongol invasions. The Crusades were a small and sordid chapter of this story, resulting in nothing but increased animosity and wasted lives. But even before, during and after the Crusades, Muslims were invading Europe from all corners, penetrating into the ivory tower, the pulpit and the minds of everyday people. They came not in armies but between the covers of books, their ideas painstakingly translated over many centuries from Arabic into Latin. They came in bolts of cloth and masterfully woven carpets. And they came in new medicines and schools that were founded on their scientific principles. Their allies were the eager European intellectuals, merchants and common people who, over the course of centuries, made Islamic culture their own.

HOLY TOLEDO

The story begins in the city that El Greco memorialized in his stunning landscape. Looking at his spiritual portrait of the city, with its grassy hills trembling in the wind, its buildings tall and stark beneath a tumultuous sky, one can feel the intensity of Toledo. Today tourists can visit its Gothic cathedral, view El Greco's *Burial of Count Orgaz*, and amble about the narrow medieval streets. If one looks closely there are remnants of an earlier age, a time when Muslims, Christians and Jews lived and learned together in this very place. Toledo was more than just the inspiration for a great painting. This was the birthplace of Western Europe's scientific revolution.

For centuries Toledo had been a part of al-Andalus. Then the caliphate disintegrated and the era of the taifas began. Soon afterwards, Toledo was conquered by Alfonso VI of Castile in 1085. In this cultured city, the Christians found a dazzling treasure-house of knowledge. Alfonso made Toledo the new capital of a kingdom where Muslim, Christian and Jewish cultures intersected, as they had for centuries in al-Andalus in war and peace.

Alfonso married a Muslim princess from Seville and made his court in the Muslims' image. Arabic words began to inflect the Castilean language. Christian courtiers and commoners alike went Arab and dressed, ate, decorated and composed in the sophisticated styles of their southern neighbors.

Toledo bloomed with cultural fertility. Visitors from all of Christendom marveled at the splendors of Islamic Spain, what one traveler called the "ornament of the world." To Europeans still immersed in the mental squalor of the dark ages, Toledo was a beacon of light. Like moths to the flame, they came.

Among them was a group of treasure-hunters. These intrepid explorers came for Toledo's most precious resource: books. Throughout the twelfth and thirteenth centuries, the great minds of Islamic civilization would be discovered and translated into Latin. Translation became a veritable industry in Toledo, supported in part by Archbishop Don Raimundo and other clerics. It was thanks to these scholars that Ibn Sina and Ibn Rushd became Avicenna and Averroes, household names in European universities.

No translator was more influential than Gerard of Cremona. Born somewhere around 1114 in his native Italy, Gerard absorbed as a youth what limited learning Europe had to offer. Bored and restless, he journeyed to Toledo where he spent the next forty years of his life translating a cornucopia of Greek and Muslim scientific works, what would become the curriculum of European students for the next four or five centuries. Thanks to him, more Arabic science entered into the Latin tongue than from any other source.

The official list of Gerard's translations from Arabic totals 87 works in the subjects of logic, philosophy, mathematics, astronomy, medicine, astrology, alchemy and geomancy (a kind of divination). The list of authors whose work he introduced to Europe is staggering: Aristotle, al-Razi, al-Kindi, Euclid, Archimedes, al-Haytham, Galen, Apollonios, Hypsicles, Theodosios, Menelaos, Ptolemy, al-Khwarizmi, al-Farghani, al-Naiziri, Thabit ibn Qurra, Ibn Sina and Abul-Qasim, to name a few. The various works amount to an encyclopedia of Islamic scientific knowledge. Thanks to Gerard's efforts, a number of technical terms were introduced into European languages, like "retina," "iris," "rhombus," and "clavicula."

Translating was a difficult and time-consuming business. It was usually accomplished by partners, one of them a bilingual Jew or Mozarab Christian who would render the work into the common tongue and another scholar who translated it into Latin. Each of these linguistic explorers had their own particular interests. Gerard desired most to read and translate Ptolemy's *Almagest*. Others like John of Seville produced Latin versions of Islamic astrology. Robert, an Englishman who became the archbishop of Pamplona, and Hermann the Dalmatian were partners employed by the church to make the first translation of the Qur'an. Robert also gave Europe al-Khwarizmi's *Algebra* and the works of al-Kindi. Hermann worked on Ptolemy's *Planisphere* and Euclid's *Elements*. Another famous pair of interfaith translators is Dominicus Gundissalinus, the archdeacon of Cuellar and his Jewish partner Avendauth or Ibn Daud. They collaborated on Ibn Sina's *De anima*, and worked separately on al-Ghazali's *Aims of the Philosophers* and Ibn Sina's *Kitab-al-Shifa*.

Elsewhere in Europe the Jews were being slaughtered or "ethnically cleansed," as was the case in England under the crusading King Richard I. But here, in this multicultural environment, Jews and

Christians worked in harmony. Through the efforts of these men and many more, the treasures of Toledo were unearthed and distributed throughout Europe.

Christians did not discover these works in the Palestine they invaded. They found them in their own backyard, remnants of a civilization that had far outshined their own. Now they gave these works to Europe as a priceless gift, the seeds of a new era. In every way, these translators of Toledo were the real Crusaders, liberating the holy land of the mind.

THE BOOK OF ROGER

Long before Italian was the official language of Sicily, the muezzin's call was heard in Palermo. In a desultory war of attrition with the Byzantines, Muslims finally won Sicily in 902 when Taormina, the last stronghold of Christian resistance, was besieged and conquered. From Sicily Muslims staged raids into mainland Italy, even sailing up the Tiber in 846 to sack Rome and loot St. Peter's. Central Italy was prone to Muslim attacks into the tenth century. For the next two hundred years, Muslims occupied sections of Apulia and Calabria, including the cities of Bari, Brindisi and Reggio. Sailing further off, they founded a colony in France, near Nice, controlling the passes to the Alps till 973.

Sicily was a multi-ethnic stew of Arabs, Lombards, Greeks, Jews, Berbers, Persians and sub-Saharan Africans. Mix in a touch of religious intolerance between Muslims and Christians, as well as Sunnis and Shias, and you have an explosion waiting to happen. Life in Islamic Sicily was never particularly stable, though one Arab traveler claimed that Sicily had more mosques than any other region in the Muslim world. A thriving trade center, Sicily lured merchants from Arabia, Egypt and the Maghrib as well as Italy. The various Muslim regimes made alliances with Naples to fight its Lombard rivals and even sided with the Byzantines against the German Emperor Otto II.

When they weren't warring with Byzantium the Muslims of Sicily were embroiled in the political conflicts of Northern Africa. A sizeable

Berber community existed on the island, which periodically revolted against its Fatimid rulers. Christians, with the eager coaxing of Constantinople, also rebelled. At the same time, Muslim Sicilians were called upon by Cairo to support their efforts in Africa or back one Fatimid against another. The drain on manpower, resources, and money began to show by the eleventh century.

As elsewhere in the Islamic world, Sicily was fatally weakened by internecine warfare. It was a perfect time for Christians to gain lost ground. By 1060, Norman warriors had occupied Messina. From there they staged a series of campaigns which resulted in the 1072 capture of Palermo. Muslims attempted a valiant resistance but in-fighting and lack of support from their co-religionists led to the final surrender in 1091.

Muslim civilization, however, was far from extinct. In fact, the Norman conquerors soon went native—none more so than Roger II, who ruled from 1111 to 1154. The new king allowed Muslims to join his court and his army, conducted diplomatic relations with the Fatimids, and kept, to the consternation of the Pope, a harem of Christian and Muslim women. The crude French warlord was clearly spellbound by his more civilized subjects.

Arab historians also praised Roger for his patronage of Muslim philosophers and scientists. The Norman ruler was especially interested in geography, a relatively underdeveloped field in medieval Europe. The man who satisfied Roger's curiosity about the world outside Sicily was Abu Abdallah Muhammad ibn Muhammad ibn Abdallah ibn Idris al-Qurtubi al-Hasani. You can understand why most scholars call him al-Idrisi.

He was born in al-Andalus in 1099, educated in Cordoba and spent many years wandering the length and breadth of Islamic civilization. The biographical details are slim since Muslim historians considered him a renegade after his move to Christendom. For reasons that may have had a great deal to do with money, al-Idrisi offered his services to Roger, dedicated his most famous work to him, and spent the rest of his life in Christian Sicily. In return for Roger's generosity, al-Idrisi gave him the world.

Muslim travelers had reached India and China by land and sea centuries before. Their trader ships had sailed along the coasts of Africa. Some had even ventured out into the mysterious Atlantic Ocean. To demonstrate Muslim geography to Roger, al-Idrisi constructed a silver planisphere which mapped the known world in startling detail.

Roger and his court were awestruck at the vastness of the continents and seas. On the orders of his patron, al-Idrisi composed a written explanation of his precious globe, loading it with economic, political and even climatic detail. This was *Nuzhat al-Mushtaq fi Ikhtiraq al-Afaq*, or The Delight of Him Who Desires to Journey through The Climates. To the Normans it was simply known as *al-Kitab al-Rujari*, Roger's Book. In one of his later volumes for Roger's son, William II, al-Idrisi created a world atlas, comprised of seventy-three separate maps. For centuries to come the Muslim geographer's wealth of information along with his highly accurate maps—based on scientific observation—would enrich and expand Christendom's knowledge of the world outside its borders.

Rules of Health

In the eleventh century the seeds of Muslim learning spread from Sicily to bear fruit on the mainland. It was in the city of Salerno, near Naples, that the European world first met the staggering discoveries of al-Razi, Ibn Sina and others. Salerno would become the first medical university in Europe. All it took was the arrival of Constantine the African.

He was born in Carthage and spent his youth traveling throughout the known world, visiting Baghdad, India, Ethiopia and Constantinople. Finally he found his way to Italy, where he became the secretary of Roger's brother, the Duke of Salerno. For years he lectured on medicine until becoming a Benedictine monk and moving to a monastery, where he died in 1087.

Most of the details of his life are legendary but it appears that Constantine was a true rara avis, a Muslim convert to Christianity. For Europe, it was a godsend: an Arabic-speaking Christian trained in the cutting-edge medical schools of the Islamic world. In no time he was hard at work translating a series of Arabic books that brought European medicine out of the Dark Ages.

With the help of a fellow Arab named John, known as "the Saracen," Constantine translated the standard medical text in the Islamic world, the *Royal Book of Ali ibn al-Abbas,* physician to the caliph. Europeans now learned of surgery, as well as how to treat hemorrhoids, nasal polyps, cataracts and infections. They studied the intricacies of the capillary system, discovered gynecology and began to practice a Muslim medical specialty: urinalysis.

Thanks to al-Razi and others, Muslim medicine considered clinical observation more trustworthy than authorities like Galen. Under Constantine's tutelage, students began the study of anatomy by dissecting pigs. Learning by leaps and bounds, pupils and professors soon made Salerno synonymous with surgery. One alumnus, Roger of Salerno, wrote the first European surgical text, thoroughly incorporating the lessons he learned from Islamic medicine.

Like a Muslim university, women were allowed to study at Salerno and the institution existed somewhat autonomously from the church. The curriculum was the same as in Baghdad, with three years devoted to general study and four more focused on medicine. The last year was spent in an internship under one of the lecturing physicians.

By the twelfth century, Salerno had compiled what became known as the *Rules of Health.* Going through one hundred forty editions the *Rules* were a series of two thousand five hundred verses designed to convey the basic concepts of modern medicine, urging readers to urinate regularly, brush their teeth, eat light suppers and get at least six hours of sleep a night.

Islamic medicine spread through Europe like wildfire. Small wonder, since it worked far better than the superstition and folk remedy on which people were forced to rely. As Europeans discovered its effectiveness, they flocked to study at Salerno and soon built similar institutions closer to home. These became the first universities, where professors began to expound upon that most precious of Muslim exports: the scientific method. It is in Salerno, far more than the city-states of Tuscany, that the Italian Renaissance truly began.

A DIFFERENT KIND OF CRUSADER

In 1194 the Normans were forced to pack their bags and vacate Sicily. The Holy Roman Empire had overrun their kingdom, ushering in a new era. Frederick II, the heir to the throne, was crowned in Palermo in 1198 when he was three years old. His mother died that year and the young king became the ward of Pope Innocent III. As King of Sicily through his boyhood, the young Frederick mastered the arts of the soldier as well as the Arabic language. For a ruler of his time (or any time, for that matter) Frederick was uniquely intellectual, devoted to philosophy and science.

In 1215 he was crowned Holy Roman Emperor after outmatching a pretender to the throne. No doubt moved by his sudden rise to power, Frederick in a fit of piety decided to take up the cross and go crusading. Christian armies, buoyed by the emperor's vow, headed to Egypt, hoping from there to stage another attempt to "liberate" their Holy Land.

Many of the Franks already in Palestine, however, had grown rich trading with the enemy. They were none too excited about this fresh wave of chain-mailed fanatics from the West. But this didn't stop the Crusaders' enthusiasm. In a surprise attack on Damietta, they managed to conquer the city. The sultan was so horrified by the victory that he died abruptly, leaving his son al-Kamil in charge.

Then something extraordinary happened. One of the Europeans asked for the fighting to stop so that he might request an audience with the new sultan. His aim was to convert the Muslims and stop the bloodshed. For three days, al-Kamil listened to the church's most beloved saint, Francesco of Assisi, preach the gospel. At the end, the sultan bid him farewell with lavish gifts (refused by Francesco) and the parting words: "Pray for me, that God may deign to show me the law and the faith that are most pleasing to him." Al-Kamil eventually relented to an exchange of Jerusalem and its surroundings if the Crusaders departed from Egypt.

But the Christians spurned Francesco's peaceful compromise. Urged on by the Byzantines, the Franks pressed for utter extermination of the infidel. At this crucial moment, Frederick characteristically failed to appear. The Crusaders quickly tired of waiting for him to arrive and honor his vow. Destroying decades of peaceful trade relations and goodwill, they prepared to assault Cairo.

This time, however, there would be no easy victory like Damietta. As the Crusaders marched in the August heat, they did not notice that the Nile River was flooding. Their armor and horses quickly became mired in mud, their progress halted. It did not take them long to decide on retreat. As soon as the army withdrew, al-Kamil ordered the dikes on the Nile destroyed. Soon the knights were marooned on an island of sludge. In the aftermath al-Kamil was exceptionally generous. Rather than hack them to ribbons, he forced them to sign a treaty, promising they would stay out of Egypt for eight years.

Meanwhile Frederick was doing some crusading of his own on home-ground. The Muslims of Sicily were in open rebellion. Their resistance had initially begun in his youth, with their refusal to pay a tax supporting the Crusades. After years of war in 1224, Frederick decided to ethnically cleanse Sicily, removing the last sixteen thousand Muslims to Lucera on mainland Italy. Unfortunately, Lucera was about as inviting as an American Indian reservation. Here the dispossessed people created an Islamic island, doomed from the very beginning, in a sea of increasingly hostile Christians. Living a tenuous existence, the citizens of Lucera were eventually targeted by the French who occupied Sicily after the Germans. In 1301 the French exterminated Lucera's population, which they called a "disease and infection."

Frederick, however, remained attracted to and fascinated by Muslim culture. The same year he ethnically cleansed Sicily he also founded the University of Naples, its intellectual heart a large collection of Arabic manuscripts. Many of his court officials were drawn from Lucera—lawyers, scholars and scientists with whom he continued his learned studies. A scandal was caused by the numerous veiled women kept in the palace. Frederick claimed they were simple serving girls, seam-stresses and the like. But the church trembled to think that the Holy Roman Emperor kept a harem like the unbelievers. Even more shocking was his creation of a private army of devoted Muslim soldiers, who practiced their faith openly while encamped with him.

In 1225, Frederick married Yolanda, heiress to the Latin Kingdom of Jerusalem—if the Christians could ever get it back. Frederick got his opportunity in 1227 when al-Kamil requested the emperor's help against his brother al-Mu'azzam, who happened to control Jerusalem. If Frederick could win Jerusalem from al-Mu'azzam, al-Kamil would recognize Christian sovereignty there. To seal the deal, al-Kamil sent Frederick a veritable zoo, including an elephant and giraffe. These fantastic beasts awed the Europeans who never in their wildest dreams would have imagined such strange creatures. Frederick was so delighted he bestowed a knightship on the Muslim envoy.

Pope Gregory was sickened by such warm relations with the enemy, as he was by Frederick's harem. The Pope was one of Christendom's most intolerant rulers. This was the man who issued decrees in 1227 demand-ing that Jews and Muslims wear distinctive dress and stay off streets during Christian holidays (of which there were legion). They were also not allowed to hold office and were certainly not permitted to pray in public. Frederick ignored these decrees, but not because he was a friend of Muslims. It was simply that he had an unabashed love for Islamic culture and wisdom as well as the astuteness to maintain amiable diplomatic ties with Muslim rulers like al-Kamil. But the Pope was not interested in Frederick's open-minded worldview. He told the emperor in no uncertain terms that if he didn't fulfill his old vow to go slaughter Saracens then he would be excommunicated. Frederick happily complied, expecting to get Jerusalem with the help of his newfound Muslim ally. Three thousand knights (including his Muslim soldiers) set sail, while Frederick stayed in Italy, feigning illness. The furious Pope immediately excommunicated him, twice for good measure.

Eventually the emperor made his way to Palestine, only to find his hopes crushed. Al-Mu'azzam was dead and al-Kamil had taken possession of Jerusalem. When Frederick asked the sultan to live up to his promise, al-Kamil replied that were he to do so now it would enrage the Muslims. The sultan was aware of Frederick's excommunication and was counting on division in their ranks. He also knew that the Christian supply ships had sunk on their way, leaving the Crusaders on the brink of starvation. Nevertheless, al-Kamil needed to save his strength for a conquest of Syria. The two rulers eventually signed a treaty that ceded control of Jerusalem and Nazareth to the Crusaders. Frederick also pledged to allow Muslims to practice their faith there and not to raise arms against the sultan. The Crusaders had won Jerusalem for a second time, without a single drop of blood being shed. It was the highpoint of the Crusades' wretched history, accomplished only through Frederick's peculiar habit of seeing Muslims through the lense of politics rather than religious bigotry.

After crowning himself in the church of the Holy Sepulcher, Frederick took a tour of the Dome of the Rock, climbing to the top of its pulpit. Unfortunately his show of religious tolerance excited admiration from neither Christians nor Muslims, who both saw the treaty as a betrayal. The highly civilized and peaceful conduct of the two rulers perished with them. In 1244 Turks overran Jerusalem, wresting it from the Crusaders for keeps.

THE SICILIAN QUESTIONS

While Frederick's Jerusalem adventure did little to alter the course of history, another crusade at home yielded magnificent results. In the midst of his tumultuous political career, Frederick was also engaged in an intellectual quest. His goal was nothing less than a complete understanding of Muslim wisdom, even at the cost of excommunication.

His court was a marvel of scientific inquiry, including a menagerie of exotic animals and a tent planetarium made of gold and precious stones, a gift from the sultan of Damascus. In this cultivated atmosphere his private faculty of Muslim scholars held forth on the whole body of Islamic knowledge. The translation of Arabic texts into Latin, begun in the eleventh century, intensified to fever pitch.

One of the foremost translators in his court was the notorious Michael Scot. As a young man, Michael left his native Scotland to mine the Muslim and Greek riches of Toledo. From there he traveled to Sicily where he became Frederick's chief translator, astrologer, physician, alchemist and, some claimed, wizard. It was in royal Palermo that Scot completed his translations of Ibn Sina, the Jewish philosopher Moses Maimonides and, most importantly, Ibn Rushd's commentaries on Aristotle's *De Anima*.

One of Ibn Rushd's most controversial tenets was the mortality of the soul. A story relates Frederick's grisly experiment to prove this hypothesis. While talking to a priest who claimed the soul was immortal, Frederick decided to nail one of the man's followers into a barrel. Sealed tight, the miserable fellow soon died of suffocation. Opening the cask, Frederick exclaimed that the soul must have died with him, since there was nowhere to which it could have escaped.

Whether the story is true or not, it reveals a dimension of Frederick's character that the church found more horrifying than any other. He was a *scientific* man, a natural skeptic who used the methods of Islamic science to threaten the sacred beliefs of Christianity. In a letter to the medical university at Salerno dated 1240, he even urged them to study anatomy by dissecting cadavers—*human ones*. Frederick knew full well that the church had outlawed this practice for centuries. He was simply unconcerned with age-old prejudices and superstitions.

So curious was Frederick about the new philosophy of Ibn Rushd that he composed what became known as the Sicilian Questions. What Frederick most wanted to know was this: Was the world eternal and could the soul, in fact, be mortal? Along with these questions were others concerning optics, Muslim theology and the hadith. These questions were circulated to al-Kamil and other Muslim luminaries until they wound up in the hands of the Almohad caliph. He referred them to a Spanish Muslim named Ibn Sabin, who composed his *Answers to Sicilian Questions,* our only remaining source for Frederick's original queries.

What fascinated the emperor was Islamic philosophy, science and religion, the very things that the church loathed and feared with every fiber of its being. The Pope excommunicated him again, claiming Frederick had denied the Virgin Birth and labeled Moses and Jesus as impostors. It could not have been too far from the truth, since even Muslim historians noted that Frederick was a materialist who only toyed with his traditional religion.

Frederick was dangerous because he was not just a humble scholar. He was the Holy Roman Emperor with the means and power to disseminate Ibn Rushd's ideas through all of Christendom. In the end, Frederick was the most successful Crusader in medieval history. Winning Jerusalem, he also spread Islamic science and philosophy through every corner of Europe. Perhaps the greatest testament to his success was Dante's *Inferno,* where we find Frederick in hell.

STRANGE BEDFELLOWS

Throughout the Middle Ages, the church had railed against the evils of the "Saracens" and "the Turk." Concurrently, Italian merchant republics had been doing a brisk trade with the enemy. Over time, the civilized tastes of the Islamic world won Christendom over, creating vast markets for its luxury goods and permanently altering European culture and cuisine.

Europeans had been trading with Muslims for centuries but in a half-hearted way. Vikings would sail down to Arabia to exchange timber and furs for gold and silver coins. Spaniards and Franks would sneak into al-Andalus and get a taste of sherbet and asparagus. Occasionally some adventurous monks would journey to the borderlands of Spain for a peek at the enemy. But early medieval Europe was still a world of isolated manors and villages. Few had the means or the ability to venture into the exotic lands of the caliphate.

This changed with the growth of towns and the merchant class in the eleventh century. Suddenly a new group of men rushed about, trying to make their fortune and show their former lords how to really live in style. Those with access to the Mediterranean had a distinct advantage. The city-states of Venice, Genoa, and Pisa were the front-runners.

The Mediterranean was the artery of civilization. Its waterways carried the riches of China to the shores of Spain. The coasts of Fatimid Egypt and the bazaars of Baghdad were the destinations of Silk Road caravans and their luxuriant textiles, spices and other delights. During the Crusades, Italian vessels were employed as ferries, supply ships and men-of-war, thus beginning a long and fruitful relationship with the Islamic coastline. To their amazement, the Italians found that the Muslims actually wanted something from them, mostly wood and iron. In exchange, the Venetians, Genoese and Pisans were only too happy to acquire pepper, sugar and other foods, raw and finished silk, glass, metalware and gems. Upon arrival in Europe they made staggering profits, enriching their private coffers and turning their puny maritime republics into major political players.

To protect their sizeable investments, the Italians initiated diplomatic ties with Egypt and Tunis in the mid-thirteenth century. The crucial ports of the Eastern Mediterranean and the Black Sea were now in the hands of the Mamluks. Both sides benefited from the trade, while ignoring whatever religious differences they might have.

That was until the Pope, incensed by the Muslim reconquest of Palestine, declared an embargo on trade with the enemy in 1291. Thanks to his meddling, the European economy, which had grown dependent on Muslim demand for wood and iron, was stymied until well into the fourteenth century.

But the Italians were not about to let the Pope interfere with their financial well-being. Venetians defied the pontiff by sending ambassadors to Egypt and Syria ten years later. From one such mission the Venetians had acquired the secrets of Syrian glass-blowing—a highly profitable technique which they monopolized for years. Even today tourists in Venice make a point of purchasing that city's distinctive glassware, descended from the traditions of Syria.

As the papal embargo wore on, goods from the Far East began to mysteriously spring up in the markets of Cyprus, where Venetian galleys would spirit them back to Europe. In an ironic twist, in the 1330s the painter Giotto based his halos on illegally-imported Mamluk plates, decorating altarpieces with Islamic designs that the church itself had banned.

Masaccio, considered the first Renaissance painter, followed suit a century later with his *Triptych of San Giovenale* in 1422. In this—his earliest work—he portrays the Madonna's head encircled by a halo which, like Giotto's, incorporates Arabic calligraphy in its design. What is remarkable is that on close examination, one can read in the Virgin's halo (in mirror image) the following Arabic words: *La ilaha il Allah, Muhammad-ur-Rasool-Allah* (There is no God but God and Muhammad is His Messenger). It is nothing less than the *Shahada*, Islam's basic statement of faith. Was the genius painter in fact a closet Muslim? Did he simply admire Arabic calligraphy, not knowing its meaning? Or was Masaccio playing a practical joke on the pompous ecclesiastical authorities? We will probably never know.

Painters were not the only ones to fall under the spell of Islamic art. During the earlier Romanesque period (1050-1200) sculpture employed an eclectic mix of styles, including Islamic. A prime example is the church of Saint-Pierre in Moissac. Beneath its famous Christ in Majesty tympanum, one can find a lintel ornamented with Islamic rosettes. Decorative scalloping, another distinctive feature of Islamic art, adorns its trumeaux.

The interiors of cathedrals also bear the sign of Islamic influence. Nave arcades were often supported by horseshoe arches, while the nave itself was framed by enormous ogival vaults. These pointed arches, so characteristic of mosque design, became the very definition of Gothic. The Cathedral of Pisa is a perfect example of the synthesis between basilica and mosque, perhaps because Pisa constructed the cathedral to commemorate an eleventh-century naval victory over a Muslim fleet. Through contact with Muslims in Sicily and al-Andalus, Christians continued to import the aesthetics of masterpieces like the Great Mosque of Cordoba to revolutionize European architecture.

Once the Crusades got started Venice, Genoa and Pisa began setting up diplomatic missions in Islamic countries, where they protected their trade privileges and supervised their fleets. The Muslims rented them whole neighborhoods where they were segregated from the native population. It was in one such embassy that Leonardo Fibonacci, the son of the Pisan ambassador, would learn the Arabic-Hindu arithmetic and accounting methods which he introduced to Europe in his 1202 book *Liber abbaci*.

Over time, trade with the Islamic world had the additional benefit of enhancing European cuisine. Muslims introduced cutting-edge irrigation techniques as well as a cornucopia of new delicacies: rice, sugarcane, mangoes, bananas, lemons, eggplants, watermelons, spinach and artichokes. While all these were delicious, there was another far more important Muslim agricultural export: *cotton*.

In the Near East and Europe, it was Muslims who first adopted cotton as a material, with Muhammad leading the way. Apparently the Prophet was fond of white cotton shirts and trousers under the old-style wool cloaks. After his death, the caliphs maintained the style, adding ever greater embellishments. Rich and poor alike used cotton for outer garments, tablecloths, funeral shrouds, curtains, rugs, veils, turbans and even underwear.

Cotton became the newest sensation in Europe and its most coveted form was *tiraz*, a Persian word meaning embroidery. Originally used to embellish official robes with an individual's title or Qur'anic verses, tiraz came to mean any embroidered garment hailing from Muslim lands. During the late medieval period and into the Renaissance, Arabic script became a stylish fad in Europe. The rich and famous could be seen parading around in their Baghdad best, the sleeves and hem proclaiming— unbeknownst to the wearer—the praises of Allah and his Prophet. The tiraz fabrics and their highly decorative lettering became the very essence of sophistication. In one Renaissance painting by Andrea Mantegna (the San Zeno altarpiece), the Virgin herself is decked out in an embroidered tiraz robe and haloed by what appears to be a Mamluk brass plate with a Qur'anic inscription. At her feet is a carpet woven in Turkey, while in the hands of a nearby saint is a finely-tooled leather book cover hailing from Muslim North Africa. Medieval was out. Muslim was in.

Venice and the Mamluks began to engage in diplomacy that was more akin to advertising. They sent each other porcelain, cloths, brassware—always the newest and the most beautiful—in the hopes that they would impress the rulers and their courtiers, thus starting a buying trend. When Ottoman Turks set up an embassy in Venice, Italian textile manufacturers presented the Turkish ambassador with their finest crimson robe, knowing full well he would wear it in his countrymen's presence, initiating the next lucrative fad.

By the fifteenth century, luxury good consumption was at fever pitch. The demand was so great that Europeans began to imitate Muslim imports, incorporating designs from Turkey, China, Persia and India. Their knock-offs became so popular and affordable that soon they were turning around and selling fifteen per cent of their products to their Muslim trading partners!

Things began to cool down when Turkey conquered Mamluk Egypt and monopolized trade in the Eastern Mediterranean. After fighting numerous wars with their former business associates, Venice floundered as an economic superpower. On the other side of Europe, Spanish and Portuguese merchants decided to find new ways to China and India, cutting out the formidable Ottoman middlemen.

Far more than the Crusades, it was this system of trade that brought Islamic luxury goods and culture into the European mainstream. The real history of interaction between the two polities was far more than a vicious military contest. It was a philosophical, scientific and cultural exchange that spanned centuries, affecting body, mind and soul.

10

Children of Abraham, Children of Aristotle

W hich brings us to the inevitable question: What happened to Islam, the civilization that gave birth to the European Renaissance? For it seems that while Europe's cultural, economic and political power grew by leaps and bounds, the world of Islam stagnated.

Today we hear scholars and other more dubious experts describe the Muslim world as the veritable antithesis of the modern, scientific, rational worldview that the West has come to call its own. To the average person in America, Muslims are stereotyped as terrorists, suicide bombers and the like who hate our way of life and want to destroy it. From political cartoons to films, Islam is portrayed as an extremist religion that is more warlike and misogynistic than any other.

This does not sound like the people who gave us al-Razi or Ibn Sina or al-Khwarizmi. If what everyone says about Islam today is true then the "what happened?" question becomes even more perplexing.

MUTAZILITES VS. ASHARITES

Scholars have called this question "the problem of Islamic decadence." The problem is explained like this: Toward the end of the Middle Ages, a fight broke out between the Mutazilites (the philosophers) and the Asharites (the theologians). After centuries of sparring, the Asharites won the contest—though how and why exactly this came to pass is never adequately explained. With the demise of Ibn Rushd, scholars claim the light of reason was extinguished. Islam rejected the rationalism of ancient Greece while Christendom embraced it. What better illustration of Islam's inherent backwardness and tendency toward narrow-minded literalism? Without philosophy, Muslims soon fell prey to the culturally superior Westerners who had the good sense to apprehend the virtue of reading Aristotle.

It's all very interesting except for one thing: *it is sheer nonsense.*

Philosophy did not extinguish itself after Ibn Rushd at all. Two hundred years later, another genius was born, this time in Tunisia. His name was Ibn Khaldun (1332-1406). While serving various Muslim rulers (including the ill-fated kingdom of Granada), Ibn Khaldun wrote a number of works on logic and Sufism. His masterpiece is *al-Muqaddimah,* a history of the world so brilliant that Bernard Lewis calls him "the greatest historical thinker of the Middle Ages." In the *al-Muqaddimah*, Ibn Khaldun invented the discipline of sociology as well as a historical methodology more sophisticated than anything that had come before. It was in this work that he originated the concept of the inevitable "rise and fall" of empires, something Europeans would not begin to explore for centuries.

If Islam was still capable of producing great thinkers, it also did not suddenly lose its ability to harness scientific know-how and apply new technology. While eschewing the printing press, the Ottoman Turks knew enough about guns to stay a major player in European politics till 1700. From 1453 onward, the Turks occupied most of Eastern Europe, built mosques and madrassahs there, gathered Renaissance artists like Gentile Bellini to their courts and fought their way into Austria on several occasions. Their carpets and ceramics became fixtures in European high society and the Janissaries, their elite military corps, were the terror of a continent.

After the Mongols and the Reconquista, Islam turned its energies eastwards. A new dynasty, the Mughals, conquered Central Asia and India and ruled there until the nineteenth century. The Mughals made India so rich that the British dedicated themselves to robbing the country of everything it was worth. Islam spread as far as the Philippines and Indonesia, which today has the largest population of Muslims in the world. Hundreds of years after the Crusades, the Islamic world took up more territory than ever.

But this paled in comparison to the vast riches of the Americas. It was there that England, France, Spain and Portugal grew wealthy from the treasure they plundered and the slaves they made first among the indigenous peoples and then the Africans. According to Jack Weatherford, the author of *Indian Givers: How the Indians of the Americas Transformed the World,* in the period between 1576 and 1650, the Spaniards looted 200 tons of gold, with a value in today's dollars of $2.8 billion. In the first fifty years of the European invasion of the Americas, $3.3 billion of silver was imported to Seville. Pizarro's annihilation of the Incas sent approximately ten million dollars' worth of booty back to Europe, curing a continent-wide depression. Sugar plantations spread across both sides of the Atlantic, making billions in today's dollars. Slaves were exported in exponential numbers to feed the insatiable European sweet-tooth. Trade monopolies such as the British East India Company and the Dutch East India Company had annual profits of three hundred percent. Weatherford writes that "new wealth in the hands of Europeans eroded the wealth of all the other countries in the world and allowed Europe to expand into an international market system." For nearly four hundred years, these European powers reaped staggering riches, making them the wealthiest nations in history. Is it surprising then that the fortunes of Europe rose as the Islamic world's declined?

It was not rationalism that made Europe superior. At the same time as the age of exploration and the scientific revolution, Europeans were burning so-called witches in droves and fighting one increasingly vicious war after another. The shift in power had little to do with intellectual or cultural factors and everything to do with cold hard cash.

The fact that Islam's fall is a "problem" at all is remarkable. After all, is the decline of Rome a "problem" for us? Or Spain? Or Great Britain?

These great empires became great by owning the lion's share of world wealth. They stopped being great when someone else took the wealth away. Empires have a fairly predictable life cycle of rise and fall. In the ultimate scheme of things, none last.

It is self-evident that a state's cultural significance assumes a greater importance the more rich and powerful it is. How many of us know any Spanish painters before Spain conquered the New World? Surely there must have been one or two. When do we ever study modern Greek art—anything made after the first century BC or so? For us Egyptian culture seems to stop after the pharaohs. Our image of Britain is mired in the Victorian world. France and fin de siècle Paris are inextricably bound together. Yet presumably before and after their fifteen minutes of wealth, these societies continued to have some kind of meaningful intellectual and cultural life.

The Islamic world was no different. For a long stretch (by history's standards) it held on to greater wealth than anyone else in the field. That wealth provided the necessary surplus to afford luxuries like philosophy and art. Countries that have less wealth, or who suffer under foreign occupation—like most of the Islamic world for the past 200 years—have more pressing concerns on their minds like survival or independence. Wealth brings a kind of freedom with it that poorer nations don't have, a freedom to think, create and discover unfettered by other concerns or demands. For a long time the Islamic world had that freedom. For a shorter time it lost that wealth and all its perks, as Italy did after 476 or England after 1945. Whether the Muslim world will retrieve some of that wealth—and create its own renaissance—is a question that is being decided in our time.

THE PROBLEM OF ORIENTALISM

If there is any problem with Islamic history, it is with some of those who write it. For these scholars Islam's decline as a cultural and political power needs to be carefully framed by the proper point of view, religiously and culturally. Indeed, the whole study of Islamic civilization itself has to be engineered so that we learn the right kinds of lessons. This historical engineering has been instrumental in silencing Islam's role in Western history. The proper name for it is *Orientalism.*

Orientalism, as Edward Said noted, is both an institution and a process by which scholars of the East, the Orient, created a history that meshed with their colonialist agendas as well as their cultural and religious prejudices. Christian polemicists thus tended to find in their study of Islam what they were looking for. In their eyes, it was an inferior faith compared to Christianity. Through poor translations of the Qur'an and misguided studies of Islamic history, they showed Islam's innate belligerence and backwardness.

Interestingly none of them seemed to notice that the adjectives "anti-modern," "fundamentalist," "bellicose," "misogynist," and the like could also be applied to European Christianity throughout the ages. The Inquisition threatened Galileo with execution four hundred years after Ibn Rushd and lasted in Spain till the nineteenth century. Christians have been killing other Christians, Jews and Muslims in Europe for centuries and still are. Christian fundamentalism is alive and well, forming a powerful political force in the United States. And despite the fact that Islam is a supposedly misogynist religion, Turkey, Pakistan and Indonesia have all elected female heads of state while predominantly Christian America has not as of this writing.

Orientalism does more than promote religious bigotry. It also serves to justify colonialism. By "forgetting" the great debt owed to Islam, Europeans could reinforce their own notions of genetic superiority. It was better to believe that their power had to do with race and religion and not with money. Every empire has the delusion that it is unlike any other, ruling not through force of arms but brilliance of mind. If they can convince themselves of that then maybe the ones they rule will begin to believe it too. That makes the business of empire that much easier.

The truth, however, can still be found if one is diligent and open-minded. Many Orientalists do their best to discourage us from this task. They bury Islamic history in heavy-as-lead prose that is as tedious to read as it is to understand. My college text on medieval Islam had nothing to do with Islam's contributions to the sciences and the arts. Forced to dwell solely on its internal political history, I came away with little more than name recognition of the Umayyads and the Abbasids. Names, Arabic jargon and bewildering geography in such works alienate the average reader from whatever information might be gathered. Islamic history becomes a boring monotone of conquests, assassinations and inconsequential battles. It is hardly surprising that I came away thinking Muslims were altogether alien and contentious, having nothing to do with my culture or history.

Islamic vs. Arabic

In contemporary scholarship, one seldom sees the joining of "Islam" or "Islamic" with words like "civilization," "literature," and so forth. While many scholars are beginning to overcome this squeamishness, many others still prefer to use terms like "Arabic literature" and "Arabic civilization" when referring to the cultural products of the Islamic Middle Ages. Their argument is that Islam did not concern itself with science and philosophy, or poetry and medicine. Instead, they claim, it is the secular Arabic language and culture that served to promote discoveries and innovations in these varied fields.

Calling this wealth of learning "Arabic" culture is to belie the many great advances made by non-Arabs. Ibn Sina was from Uzbekistan. Al-Razi and al-Ghazali were Persians. Salah al-Din was a Kurd. Qutuz was a Mamluk Turk. Over a thousand years, power passed from Umayyads to Abbasids to Fatimids to Seljuks to Kurds to Mamluks to Ottomans. What bound all these diverse people together was not their common use of Arabic as a language but their profession of the Prophet's faith. Indeed, it was the Qur'an that made Arabic an international language and Islam's tolerance of other cultures that, more than anything, made the House of Wisdom possible.

By excising "Islamic" from anything having to do with rationality, scholars and other writers hide the fact that it was Muslims who first found worth in Greek philosophy, Muslims who studied it and Muslims who debated the uses to which it should be put. To separate the cultural accomplishments of Muslims from their faith is a ridiculous decontextualization, akin to ignoring the fact that Michelangelo's frescoes happen to be in the Vatican. This truth flies in the face of works like Richard Stark's *The Victory of Reason,* which claims Christianity alone among religions encourages "rational exploration." As anyone can see from looking at the historical record, the spread of Islam among the Arabs and Persians acted as a galvanizing agent for the mind. With its practical appreciation of the physical world as well as the spiritual one, Islam placed a creative emphasis on nature that medieval Christianity did not.

CHILDREN OF ABRAHAM, CHILDREN OF ARISTOTLE

Most school children in America know little about European history or culture. One thing, however, that they are sure to encounter somewhere along the way is the history of the Italian Renaissance.

The Renaissance is the West's creation myth. It is there in Florence, we learn, that the Middle Ages ended and the rebirth of classical ideals began. The result was humanism, rationalism, enlightenment—everything that makes us culturally superior to everyone else.

It is important for everyone to understand that these are European traits, derived from the Greeks. We are their only direct descendants. As the Orientalist J. J. Saunders put it, "The Muslims did, as we have seen, borrow a good deal from Greece, but in a limited and indirect fashion: the Greek past never belonged to them in the sense in which it did to Christendom."

This is the crux of the myth. How strange it would be for Ibn Rushd to read that passage. Or Ibn Sina. Or the translators at the House of Wisdom. Or al-Razi. Or any of the other countless and anonymous Muslim scholars who were buying Aristotle in bookstores when Europeans had forgotten how to read.

They would tell you that the Greeks belonged to Islam as much as they ever belonged to Christendom. They would remind you that it was they who saved the Greeks when the Christians were burning them. It was they who translated them, debated them, commented on them and improved upon their systems. Muslims gave Western Christians their science, their medicine, their music, their food, their clothes, their poetry, their philosophy and their mathematics. They were the ones who thrust Europe out of the Dark Ages and into the Enlightenment. This is the terrible secret that the Renaissance myth tries to hide.

We must begin learning history by *un*learning the cultural "truths" we have been taught about Islam. These paradigms have nestled in the muck of our collective unconscious for centuries. Born of religious intolerance, they slowly cemented themselves as Islam became an increasing political and cultural threat. It was because Islam was so successful that our culture made it seem like a failure. It was because we owed Muslims so much that we pretended we owed them nothing. For without this myth of a superior religion and a superior culture, what did we have that we could call our own?

Only something far greater, far more complex and transcendent —*a shared history of faith and culture.* The Islamic world and the "West" are (and always have been) an intricately-bound system of cultural and religious interaction. They are not separate entities as much as they are parts of an ongoing process of debate and exchange.

It is time for memory to triumph over collective amnesia. Islam belongs to the West as much as the Egyptians or the Greeks. We are the heirs of Ibn Rushd and al-Razi as much as we are the heirs of Plato and Hippocrates. And the West belongs to Islam, a rich part of its own history that has only begun to be written. It is in the writing of that new history that we might finally unlearn what has pulled us apart and learn anew what we share as children of Abraham and Aristotle.

Appendix 1

What the Qur'an Says

ON GOD

Say: "He is God, the One and Only; God, the Eternal, the Absolute. He begets not, nor is He begotten. None is like Him." Q 112:1-4

ON ANGELS

"Surely there are kind and honorable angels to protect you—writing down your deeds. They know and understand all that you do." Q 82:10-12

ON JUDGMENT

"One day the Earth will be changed to a different Earth and so will be the Heavens. Men will be led forth before God, the One, the Irresistible. And you will see the Sinners that day bound together in fetters, their garments of liquid pitch and their faces covered with fire. God will reward each soul what it deserves." Q 14: 48-51

ON LOVE

"And among His Signs is this: that He created for you mates from among yourselves, that you may dwell in tranquility with them, and he has put love and mercy between your hearts." Q 30:21

ON JESUS

"We sent Jesus the son of Mary, confirming the Torah that had come before him. We sent him the Gospel, in which was guidance and light." Q 5:46

ON MERCY

"God is most merciful to those who show mercy." Q 12:64

ON SIN

"Truly God does not wrong anyone; they wrong themselves."
Q 10:44

ON FREE WILL

"God will never change the condition of a people until they change it themselves." Q 13: 11

ON RESURRECTION

"Man says: 'What! When I am dead, shall I then be raised up alive?' Doesn't he remember that We created him before out of nothing?" Q 19:66-67

Appendix 2

Arabic Words in English

Admiral

Adobe

Albatross

Alchemy

Alcohol

Alcove

Aldebaran

Alembic

Alfalfa

Algebra

Algorithm

Alkali

Amalgam

Amber

Amulet

Apricot

Arsenal

Artichoke

Assassin

Atlas

Azimuth

Baboon

Balcony

Banana

Baroque

Benzine

Betelgeuse

Bismuth

Borax

Cable

Calibre

Camel

Camphor

Candy

Caper

Carafe

Carat

Carmine

Carob

Check

Checkmate

Chemistry

Cheque

Chess

Chiffon

Coffee

Cotton

Coffer

Crimson

Cumin

Cupola

Cypher

Date

Demijohn

Divan

Drug

Elixir

Fanfare

Fellah

Fret (of guitar)

Frieze

Gauze

Gazelle

Gazette

Gibraltar

Ginger

Giraffe

Guitar

Gypsum

Hashish

Hazard

Henna

Hooka

Jar

Jasmine

Jumper

Julep

Lacquer

Lapis-Lazuli

Lilac

Lemon

Lute

Magazine

Marzipan

Mask

Mattress

Minaret

Monsoon

Mosque

Mulatto

Mummy

Musk

Musket

Muslin

Myrrh

Nadir

Nitre

Orange

Racket

Ream

Rice

Risk

Rocket

Rook

Saccharin

Safari

Saffron

Sandalwood

Sapphire

Satin

Sherbet

Sofa

Spinach

Sugar

Sultan

Syrup

Tabby

Talc

Talisman

Tambourine

Tariff

Tarot

Troubadour

Vizier

Zenith

Zero

Further Reading

This book was never intended to be the last word on any of its myriad subjects. Rather it should serve as an introduction, a first glimpse into a new world of history and understanding. The following texts, all used in my research, are presented for the interested reader who wishes to learn more about the shared heritage of the children of Abraham and Aristotle.

THE ORIGINS OF ISLAM

Of course every Muslim would like to read the Qur'an in Arabic and millions upon millions do. For non-Arabic speakers, there are numerous translations of the Qur'an in English. The reader should be careful, however, for not all translations are equal. N. J. Dawood's well-known Penguin edition (1956) distorts the meaning of many a verse to favor the usual violent and misogynist picture of Muslims. A prime example is the rendering of Q 2:223. In Dawood's edition we find it translated as: "Women are your fields: go, then, into your fields whence you please. Do good works and fear God." Meanwhile another translation (Abdullah Yusuf Ali's *The Holy Qur'an: Translation and Commentary* [Amana Corporation, 1983]) has a completely different tenor: "Your wives are as a tilth unto you; so approach your tilth when or how ye will; but do some good act for your souls beforehand and fear God..." The way Dawood writes, one might think all Muslim women are harem girls and pleasure slaves—a typical Orientalist view. But the verse does not concern women in general but rather wives and when sexual relations are permissive. Wives are not simply proper-ty but tilths—parcels of land that farmers sow and reap in due season and with great care. Clearly, the purpose is to demonstrate that sexual relations are not to be avoided but instead should be taken seriously, even reverentially. With a poor translation, however, this passage can become not only perplexing but offensive in a way that it was never meant to be.

A good rule of thumb is to avoid any new book with the word "Koran" in the title (like Dawood's). This old-style transliteration is often (but not always) a sign of old-school scholarship, if not anti-Islamic bias. An egregious example of this is Michael Cook's *The Koran: A Very Short Introduction* (Oxford University Press, 2000), a polemical work which conveys next to nothing of the actual nature of the Qur'an itself. For that one must consult Ali's translation as well as Michael Sells' *Approaching the Qur'an: The Early Revelations* (White Cloud Press, 1999), which contains the earliest surahs, along with penetrating analysis. Thomas Cleary's recent *The Qur'an: A New Translation* (Starlatch, 2004) is another excellent version.

To learn more about the Prophet Muhammad the best sources are his sayings, the hadith. Thomas Cleary, in his *The Wisdom of the Prophet* (Shambala, 2001), presents a selection of hadith which portray Muhammad's genius, compassion and wit. *Muhammad: A Biography of the Prophet* by Karen Armstrong (Harper San Francisco, 1992), is a readable and balanced account of the Prophet's life. Yahyah Emerick's biography *Muhammad* (Pearson, 2002) is both pious and perceptive. Maxime Rodinson's *Muhammad* (New Press, 2002) is a critical introduc-tion to the Prophet's life that combines the best and worst features of Orientalist scholarship. *Jesus and Muhammad: The Parallel Sayings* by Joey Green (Seastone, 2003) is a tiny but enlightening volume that puts Islam's prophet into perspective, drawing connections between the world's most popular religions.

The early political history of Islam is the subject of many a tome, including J. J. Saunders' *A History of Medieval Islam* (Routledge, 1965) which manages to transcend its author's Orientalist leanings (at least until the last chapter). Jonathan Bloom and Sheila Blair's *Islam: A Thousand Years of Faith and Power* (TV Books, 2000) is the well-researched and comprehensive tie-in to the wonderful PBS video series *Islam: Empire of Faith*. Bloom's article "Revolution by the Ream, A History of Paper" (Saudi Aramco World, May/June 1999) provided substantial information on the cultural output of this era. Estelle Whelan's article "Forgotten Witness: Evidence for the Early Codification of the Qur'an" (*Journal of the American Oriental Society*, 1998, Vol. 118, pp. 1-14) provided a fascinating look into the early history of the Qur'an. *A History of the Arab Peoples* by Albert Hourani (Harvard UP, 1991) is a standard reference work but perhaps even more useful are Philip K. Hitti's two volumes *Islam: A Way of Life* (U of Minnesota P, 1970) and *Makers of Arab History* (St. Martin's Press, 1968). *Islam: From the Prophet Muhammad to the Capture of Constantinople*, edited by Bernard Lewis (Oxford UP, 1987) is a two-volume collection of primary source material. For the visual learners among us, Ziauddin Sardar's *Introducing Muhammad* (Totem, 1994, with Zafar Abbas Malik) is an entertaining and amazingly informative comic book covering not only the early history of Islam but also its perception in the West. Sardar's *The No-Nonsense Guide to Islam* (Verso, 2004, with Merryl Wyn Davies) is a slightly more in-depth introduction without the graphics.

FRANKS AND MONGOLS

Medievalists have spilled oceans of ink on the Crusades. It is one of the few events in medieval history that everyone seems to know about (and now you should know why!). The best places to find primary source material on the Muslim view of 1096 and its aftermath are *Arab Historians of the Crusades* by Francesco Gabrieli (U of California P, 1969) and *The Crusades through Arab Eyes* by Amin

Maalouf (Schocken Books, 1985). For a general overview, try Karen Armstrong's penetrating analysis of the period: *Holy War: The Crusades and Their Impact on Today's World* (Anchor Books, 2001). For a more traditional European point of view, Steven Runciman's *A History of the Crusades* (Cambridge UP, 1953) remains the standard.

The Mongol invasion of Europe is one of the forgotten chapters of medieval history. Most European history texts barely mention it. For a detailed introduction some fine sources are *The Devil's Horsemen: The Mongol Invasion of Europe* by James Chambers (Cassell Publishers, Ltd, 1988) and S. R. Turnbull's *The Mongols* (Osprey Publishing, 1980). Robert Marshall's *Storm from the East: From Genghis Khan to Khubilai Khan* (U of California P, 1993) is a lavishly illustrated volume that covers not just Batu's campaign in Eastern Europe but the entire rise and fall of Chingiz and his descendants. It is also a tie-in for an informative and beautifully-shot documentary series of the same title. Michael Praudin's *The Mongol Empire: Its Rise and Legacy* (MacMillan and Co., 1940) is an older but still solidly-researched history.

To go deeper into the subject, one must consult more scholarly and inaccessible volumes. I found the work of Denis Sinor especially helpful in this regard. His *Inner Asia and its Contacts with Medieval Europe* (Variorum Reprints, 1977) has numerous articles (some of which are only in French) on Hungarian relations with the Mongols as well as Mongol military history. For English-only speakers, J. J. Saunders's posthumous book *Mongols and Muslims: Essays on Medieval Asia* (U of Canterbury, 1977) contains an informative account of the Battle of Ain Jalut and its aftermath as well as the effect of the Mongol invasions on the world of Islam. Another well-researched article is David Tschanz's "The Mongols Meet Their Match: The Battle of Ain Jalut" (http://www.strategy-page.com/articles/default.asp?target=mongol.htm).

MUSLIM MEDICINE AND SCIENCE

While most medievalists have known of Islam's incredible contributions to European civilization, few have undertaken to write about them. This job is usually left to historians of science. The groundbreaking work in this regard was done by George Sarton, who in a series of volumes including his encyclopedic *Introduction to the History of Science* (Carnegie Institution of Washington, 1931), detailed the work of such forgotten geniuses as al-Haytham and al-Razi. Seyyed Hossein Nasr's *Science and Civilization in Islam* (Harvard UP, 1968) is a remarkable compendium that combines historical analysis with primary source material. It is one of the few places where excerpts from the original works of al-Razi, al-Khwarizmi and al-Haytham can be read in English translation. Another is A. J. Arberry's translation of al-Razi's *Spiritual Physick* (John Murray, 1950).

The contributions of Muslim science are so vast that so far no one has written a single exhaustive work on the subject. Instead we have a variety of fascinating books on more specialized subjects such as *Islamic Technology: An Illustrated History* by Ahmad Y. al-Hassan and Donald R. Hill (Cambridge UP/UNESCO, 1986) which covers diverse topics like sword and glass-making, ship construction, tools, hydrology and bookbinding. Dick Teresi's *Lost Discoveries: The Ancient Roots of Modern Science, from the Babylonians to the Maya* (Simon & Schuster, 2002) highlights the debt Copernicus owed to al-Tusi. *The Norton History of Astronomy and Cosmology* by John North (W.W. Norton, 1995) details not just the work of al-Tusi but also the astronomers of medieval Spain and Baghdad. Arthur Castiglioni's *A History of Medicine* (Alfred A. Knopf, 1946) has numerous illustrations and primary source material along with a comprehensive look at how al-Razi, Ibn Sina and others revolutionized first Islamic and then European medicine. David Tschanz's article "The Arab Roots of European Medicine" (*Aramco World* May/June 1997) is an informed introduction to the same topic.

For primary source material on Islamic philosophy, I consulted Gary E. Kessler's *Voices of Wisdom: A Multicultural Philosophy Reader* (Wadsworth, 2004), which reprints an excerpt from al-Ghazali's *Deliverance from Error*. A complete text of Ibn Rushd's incendiary commentary on Plato's masterpiece can be found in *Averroes on Plato's "The Republic,"* translated by Ralph Lerner (Cornell UP, 1974). Caroline Stone's article on Ibn Rushd, "Doctor, Philosopher, Renaissance Man" (*Saudi Aramco World*, May/June 2003), provides an informative and beautifully illustrated introduction to the life of the great "Commentator."

A Shared Culture

Even general surveys will mention from time to time the impact of Italian trade with the Islamic world. *Cathedral, Forge and Waterwheel: Technology and Invention in the Middle Ages* by Frances and Joseph Gies (Harpercollins, 1994) discloses the contributions of Muslims to agriculture, military engineering, glass-making, and textiles. By far the most impressive and well-researched volume on the subject is *From Bazaar to Piazza: Islamic Trade and Italian Art, 1300-1600* by Rosamond E. Mack (U of California P, 2001), a comprehensive and extensively illustrated account of just how much Renaissance style was imported from Egypt, Syria and Istanbul. Jerry Brotton's *The Renaissance Bazzar: From the Silk Road to Michelangelo* (Oxford UP, 2002) is another well-researched and engagingly-written revision of the Renaissance myth. The National Gallery of Art in Washington has published a guide to its collection entitled *Artistic Exchange: Europe and the Islamic World* (2004) which illustrates the connection between the Renaissance and the Muslim world. Set a little to the south of Renaissance Tuscany, Aziz Ahmad's *A History of Islamic Sicily* (Edinburgh UP, 1975) provides just about the only extensive information in English on this forgotten corner of the Muslim world.

To learn more about al-Andalus, make the work of Maria Rosa Menocal your starting point. *The Ornament of the World: How Muslims, Jews and Christians Created a Culture of Tolerance in Medieval Spain* (Little, Brown and Company, 2002) is her popular and readable account of the medieval convivencia which brought light to Europe's Dark Ages. *The Arabic Role in Medieval Literary History: A Forgotten Heritage* (U of Pennsylvania P, 1987) by the same author, is a more scholarly and insightful work that not only explains the literary interaction between medieval Muslims and Christians but also how the memory of that encounter was either erased or distorted during the Renaissance. One of Menocal's own sources is the seminal work of Miguel Asin Palacios. His *Islam and the Divine Comedy* (Frank Cass & Co Ltd, 1968) remains the definitive work on the subject and is as shocking and revelatory a read today as it was when he originally published it nearly a century ago. "Flight of the Blackbird" by Robert W. Lebling, Jr. (Saudi-Aramco World July/August 2003), is an excellent and entertaining article about Ziryab.

For further information I consulted *Andalus: Spain under the Muslims* by Edwyn Hole (Robert Hale Ltd., 1958) which provided me not only with more tidbits on Ziryab but also the cultural life of al-Andalus at its peak. Henry George Farmer's essay "The Music of Islam" (in the *New Oxford History of Music, Vol. 1: Ancient and Oriental Music,* ed. Egon Wallesz, Oxford UP, 1966) provided ample evidence of the Islamic impact on Western music. For readings in the literature of Muslim Spain, the two best sources are *Anthology of Islamic Literature: From the rise of Islam to modern times,* edited by James Kritzeck (Holt, Rinehart and Winston, 1964) and *Night and Horses and the Desert: An Anthology of Classical Arabic Literature,* edited by Robert Irwin (Overlook Press, 1999). Another book by Irwin, *The Arabian Nights: A Companion* (I.B. Tauris, 2004) reveals not only the world that inspired the Nights but also how these tales in turn inspired Western literature.

Finally, there are a variety of books, many of them published recently, which seek to explain "what went wrong" with Islam and why it is a threat to world peace, our way of life, etc. Most of these simply transform prejudice into scholarship. A great many anti-Islam polemics and websites are funded by decidedly biased foundations and organizations. Know who you're getting your information from and beware of their self-interest. The two seminal works on anti-Islamic bias are Edward Said's verbally dense *Orientalism* (Vintage, 1978) and the more accessible *Covering Islam* (Vintage, 1997).

It's only fair to point out that some of the scholars I've drawn my information from are Orientalists. While many Orientalists should be credited for their exceptional scholarship, some of the most influential of them actively despise Islam as well as its many adherents for political and/or religious reasons. My hope has always been that a new era is dawning where control over history will pass from the hands of hate into the collective arms of brother and sisterhood. Let us make it so.

Index